CONTENTS

Kitchen Repairs Made Easy

A kitchen's daily ration of heavy traffic and hard use frequently leads to drooping cabinets, scratched countertops, and marred floors. Instead of replacing worn items with new ones, you can often restore them to near-original condition with the simple repairs shown on the following pages.

Self-Latching Cabinet Hinge →

Mending Kitchen Cabinets

Cabinets are an indispensable component of any kitchen; they keep pots and pans, dinnerware, utensils, and foodstuffs close at hand but out of the way until needed. Because of their constant use, however, they are prone to a variety of ailments.

Over time, the cabinet frame can twist—or rack—under its heavy load. Inserting shims—thin pieces of wood—between the cabinet and the wall may be enough to push a racked cabinet back into square, but usually it must be taken down and repaired *(right)*. While the cabinet is off the wall, the joints should be reinforced to strengthen the frame.

Removing Cabinets: Newer cabinets are screwed to the wall through hanging bars—pieces of wood attached to the upper, and often the lower, cabinet back. Screws will be visible inside, but the hanging bar is usually hidden behind it.

Older cabinets without hanging bars are most often nailed to the wall through the inside of the cabinet. To take them down, gently pry the outside edges of the cabinet with a pry bar until it is $\frac{1}{2}$ inch away from the wall, then push the cabinet back against the wall to expose nailheads.

Reinforcing Shelves: Shelves can become bowed under the weight of stacks of dishes or canned goods. In many cabinets, the shelves are removable and need only be turned over. For fixed shelves *(page 10)*, a wooden partition will provide permanent support, but remember that all shelves beneath it must be similarly braced or the sag will be transferred downward. In cabinets with a center stile, wooden strips attached to the back of the stile and the back of the cabinet can support the sagging shelf without taking up valuable space inside the cabinet.

Drawers and Hinges: The moving parts of the cabinet are particularly susceptible to wear. Drawers are most likely to break down at points of special strain—bottoms, backstops, and guides. In many drawers, you can remove the back, slide a damaged bottom out, and replace it. If intricate joints prevent this, measure the bottom, cut a piece of $\frac{1}{4}$-inch luan plywood to size, and glue it on top of the damaged bottom.

Door hinges can work loose, and the doors themselves sometimes warp out of shape. If not too severely bowed, the door can be straightened with an oak brace.

 **TOOLS**

Pry bar
Bar clamps
$\frac{1}{4}$- or $\frac{3}{8}$-inch power drill
Hacksaw
Chisel
Rabbet plane
Block plane
Utility knife

 **MATERIALS**

Wood shims
Carpenter's glue
Masking tape
Hardwood dowels
Wire brads
Angle braces
Metal center drawer glides
$1\frac{1}{4}$-inch dry-wall screws

SQUARING A RACKED FRAME

1. Straightening the cabinet.

◆ First, remove the doors; then, with a helper supporting the cabinet, detach it from the wall, saving the screws and any shims that fall. If working alone, read the box on page 14 before removing the cabinet.

◆ Glue any joints that have popped open. If they are not open enough to apply glue, tap them apart with a hammer and wood block.

◆ Close the joints with two bar clamps set near the ends of the top and bottom rail as shown in the picture below. Protect the finish by placing pieces of scrap wood between the cabinet and the bar clamps.

◆ Before the glue dries, make sure that the cabinet is square. Hook a tape measure on one corner of the cabinet and measure diagonally to the opposite corner, then measure the other diagonal *(below)*. If the measurements differ, loosen the clamps, and with a helper, gently push the two corners that are farther apart toward each other. Remeasure the diagonals and repeat the adjustment until the measurements are equal. Retighten the clamps and let the glue dry.

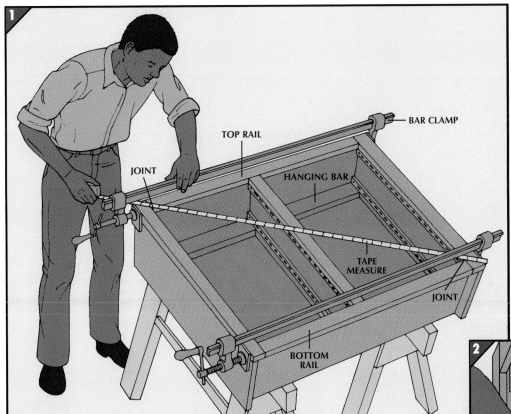

2. Strengthening the joints.

If your cabinet has protruding shelf supports on the inside frame that extend the full height of the cabinet, install metal angle braces *(top of diagram)* near the front and back of the cabinet. If the shelf supports are recessed or stop short of the corner *(bottom of diagram)*, position a 1- by 1-inch wood block at each joint.

◆ Cut the block as long as the depth of the shelf.

◆ With the block flush against the joint, drill three pilot holes *(right)* through one side of the block and into the cabinet.

◆ Then, without intersecting those three holes, drill three more pilot holes through the other side of the block.

◆ Apply glue to the remaining two sides of the block, those that rest against the cabinet. Press the block into place with the pilot holes properly aligned, then drive a $1\frac{1}{4}$-inch dry-wall screw into each pilot hole.

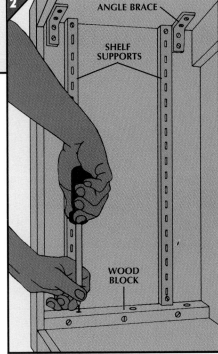

SUPPORT FOR A SAGGING SHELF

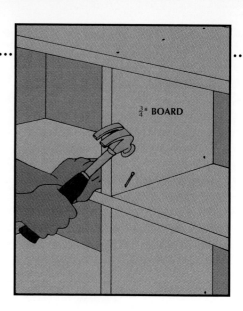

A shelf partition.
Always work from the bottom up. When each partition is inserted, the wood grain should be vertical to match the sides of the cabinet.

◆ First, measure the depth of the cabinet's shelves and cut a $\frac{3}{4}$-inch board along the grain to this measurement.

◆ At the side of the cabinet where the shelves meet the frame, measure the distance between the two lowest shelves, and cut the $\frac{3}{4}$-inch board

across the grain to that length.

◆ At the centerline of the cabinet, insert a partition between the bottom two shelves, and drive three nails straight through the shelf into the top of the partition.

◆ Near the bottom of the partition, drive two nails at a 45° angle through each side of the partition into the shelf below *(right)*.

◆ Working upward toward the shelf that is sagging, repeat for the remaining shelves.

Center stile cabinets.
As with the partition method described above, all the shelves beneath the sagging shelf must be supported.

◆ At one end of the cabinet, measure the distance between the bottom two shelves and cut two 1-by-2 pieces of wood to that length.

◆ Wedge one piece behind the center stile and the other against the center of the back of the cabinet directly opposite the stile.

◆ Drill two pilot holes through both pieces of wood and into the cabinet frame about 1 inch from each end. Drive a $1\frac{1}{4}$-inch wood screw into each hole.

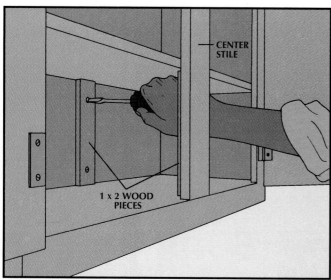

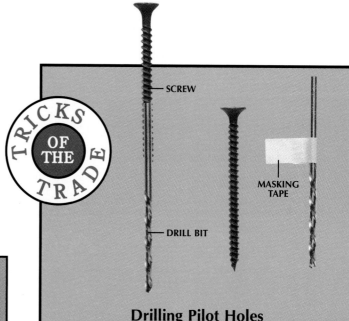

Drilling Pilot Holes

Small pieces of wood tend to split when screws are driven into them. Drilling pilot holes first makes it much easier to seat screws properly.

A pilot hole must be slightly narrower than the screw. Hold a drill bit at eye level directly in front of the screw. The screw's shank should be hidden by the bit but the threads should be visible *(above, left)*. To measure the proper depth for the pilot hole, mark the bit with a piece of masking tape about $\frac{2}{3}$ the length of the screw.

In many cases you will want to countersink the screws—that is, drive them flush with, or even below, the surface of the wood. Combination bits, available in a variety of sizes, will drill the pilot hole and the countersink hole at the same time.

Redrilling screw holes for hinges.
◆ If the hinges are loose, try tightening the screws. If a screw won't tighten, the hole is stripped and must be plugged, then redrilled.
◆ Unscrew the door from its hinges, and remove any hinge where holes in the cabinet frame need to be plugged. Save the screws.
◆ With a hacksaw, cut pieces of a hardwood dowel to the length of the screws, then splinter them with a chisel. Squirt glue into the stripped screw holes, and plug them tight with the hardwood splinters (*inset*), tapping them with a hammer to ensure a tight fit. Wipe off any excess glue.
◆ Let the glue dry, then drill pilot holes into the plugs (*right*) and re-mount the door to the cabinet with the old screws. Close it and see if it is properly aligned with the cabinet. If necessary, loosen the screws slightly, shift the door, and then retighten the screws.

HARDWOOD DOWEL

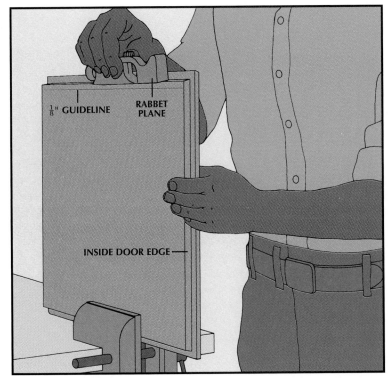

⅛" GUIDELINE RABBET PLANE

INSIDE DOOR EDGE

Planing an edge that sticks.
◆ On the inner side of the door, mark a line $\frac{1}{8}$ inch from the edge that rubs. Secure the door in a vise.
◆ On a lipped door *(left)*, use a rabbet plane or a block plane to shave the inside edge down to the marked line.
◆ On a flush door, use a block plane. Take special care not to shave the outside edge to avoid creating a gap between the closed door and the frame of the cabinet.

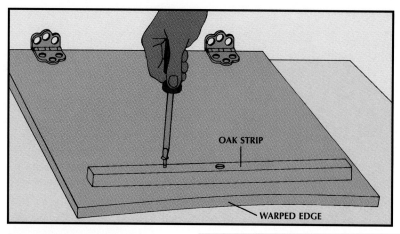

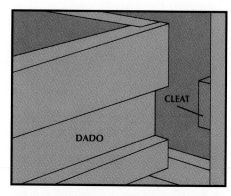

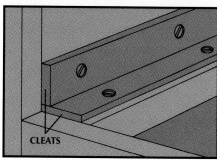

Bracing a warped door.

◆ Cut a 1-by-1 piece of oak 2 inches shorter than the length of the warped edge of the door. Set the door facedown, and center the strip 1 inch in from the warped edge.

◆ With a combination bit, drill a pilot hole through the center of the oak strip and into the door. Countersink a $1\frac{1}{2}$-inch No. 6 screw through the strip,

but do not tighten it.

◆ Working toward the edges, drill pilot holes, and countersink screws one at a time at 6-inch intervals along the strip. To avoid cracking the door, attach the 1-by-1 strip fairly loose at first, then gradually tighten the screws, starting in the center.

◆ When the warp is removed, unfasten the strip, glue it in place, and rescrew it to the door.

Replacing wooden drawer guides.

Some drawers have grooves—or dadoes—along the sides (above, top) that fit a cleat attached to the cabinet, while others slide on two cleats (above) that form a guide for the drawer's lower edges.

◆ To replace a damaged guide of either type, first trace its outline onto the cabinet with a pen or pencil. At the edge of the outline, mark the positions of the screw holes, then remove the screws. Dislodge a glued guide by gently tapping it with a hammer.

◆ Using the old guide as a template, cut a duplicate piece, then glue it to the cabinet at the traced position. Drill pilot holes for new screws, taking care to offset them about $\frac{1}{2}$ inch from the old screw holes, and secure the block with screws.

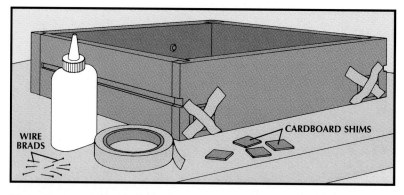

New stops on flush drawers.

◆ First, remove the worn or damaged stop blocks, then push the drawer in as far as it will go, and measure the gap between the cabinet face and the drawer front.

◆ Cut two blocks 1 inch square and slightly thinner than the measured distance, and tape them to the drawer back in place

of the old stop blocks (above).

◆ Replace the drawer and test the fit. If necessary, insert cardboard shims between the drawer back and the wood blocks until the drawer front is flush with the cabinet face.

◆ Glue the stops and shims to the drawer, then gently hammer in wire brads.

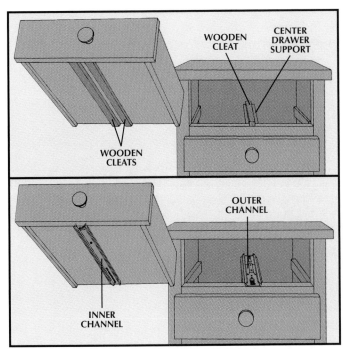

A substitute for wooden bottom guides.

If a wooden center cleat breaks, replace it with metal center guides, which come in sizes to fit most drawers and are more durable.

◆ Gently pry off the wooden cleats from the bottom of the drawer and from the center support *(left, top)*.

◆ Measure the drawer depth, and buy a metal center guide to match it.

◆ Draw a line down the center of the drawer bottom and the center drawer support.

◆ Attach the inner channel to the drawer bottom, and the outer channel to the center drawer support *(left, bottom)*.

ANCHORING A CABINET TO STUDS

1. Shimming the top of the cabinet.

◆ Check the old screw holes in the studs to make sure they are not stripped. If necessary, plug the holes and redrill them *(page 11)*.

◆ While a helper holds the back of the cabinet against the wall, using old paint lines or other markings as a guideline, check the cabinet's vertical and horizontal alignment with a level. If there is no one available to help hold the cabi-

net, see the box on page 14.

◆ If the top of the cabinet must move out from the wall, insert a shim (use the old ones if you have them) at each stud, and tap it down until the cabinet is plumb.

◆ If the cabinet is already plumb, use shims only to fill any gap at the studs between the cabinet and the wall, gently tapping them into place without moving the cabinet.

A Substitute for Another Pair of Hands

If there is no helper available to steady the cabinet against the wall while you remove or rehang it, a prop constructed of four pieces of $\frac{3}{4}$-inch plywood will serve nicely. One horizontal piece supports the cabinet bottom while the other provides a broad, sturdy base on the countertop. The two vertical pieces that bear the cabinet's weight are screwed together at right angles for added stability. Slide the prop under the cabinet, and insert shims, if needed, until it fits snugly between the cabinet bottom and the countertop.

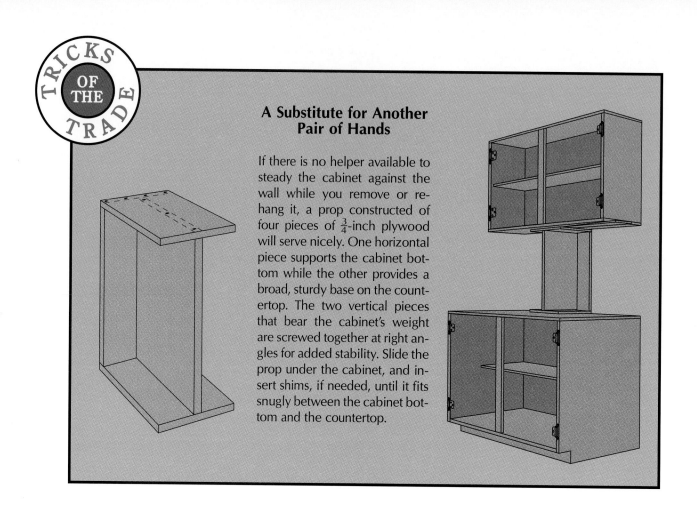

HANGING BAR

SHIMS

2. Plumbing the cabinet bottom.
◆ Drive screws into the studs through the top hanging bar, cabinet back, and shims *(left)*.
◆ If the cabinet must move out at the bottom, install shims at each stud as you did for the top.
◆ If your cabinet has a lower hanging bar *(not shown)*, shim any gap at the studs between the cabinet back and the wall, then attach it as you did the top hanging bar.
◆ Trim all the protruding shims with a handsaw or utility knife; cut almost to the wall, then snap off the waste.

Fixing Damaged Countertops

Although countertop surfaces—plastic laminate, ceramic tile, or hardwood butcher block—are strong and durable, daily use and accidents eventually take their toll. But much damage to most surfaces can be repaired.

Quick Repairs for Minor Damage: Scratches and gouges in laminate can be hidden with a matching plastic seam filler, available from countertop fabricators. Broken or lifted edges can be reglued. Stains on butcher block can usually be scraped or sanded away.

With care, a cracked ceramic tile can be removed and replaced without marring the surrounding tiles. Scrape away old grout around the edges of the tile with a grout saw. A damaged tile at the edge of the sink presents special problems; you must remove the sink *(page 102)* and cut the new tile to fit *(pages 108-109)*.

Replacing a Section of Countertop: Extensive damage to a laminate countertop can be cut out and replaced with an inset of heat-proof glass—available as a kit from home-supply centers—or ceramic tiles. Since the metal-rimmed glass inset requires that the countertop be cut through, check for braces or crosspieces under the countertop before proceeding.

To install a tile inset, remove the damaged area with a router and a $\frac{3}{8}$-inch double-fluted bit. To determine the depth of the cut, add $\frac{1}{4}$ inch for a plywood underlayment to the thickness of your tiles, then subtract $\frac{1}{32}$ inch so that the tiles will sit slightly higher than the surface of the countertop.

 **TOOLS**

Putty knife
Steel scraper
Orbital sander
Saber saw with laminate blade
Router
$\frac{3}{8}$-inch double-fluted bit
C clamp

Electric drill with $\frac{1}{4}$-inch bit
$\frac{1}{4}$-inch masonry bit
Utility knife with laminate blade
Grout saw
Pry bar
Cold chisel
Notched trowel

 **MATERIALS**

Plastic seam filler
$\frac{1}{4}$-inch plywood
Silicone caulk
Grout
Silicone sealer

Ceramic tiles
Carpenter's glue
Epoxy-based or acrylic tile adhesive

 SAFETY TIPS

Protect your eyes with goggles when using a hammer and chisel, power saw, sander, or router. Never start the router with the bit touching the surface to be routed. Wear rubber gloves when handling tile adhesive.

A quick fix for countertop scratches.
◆ Squeeze a small quantity of plastic seam filler onto a plastic plate, and work it with a clean putty knife until it begins to thicken.
◆ Wipe the scratch with a cloth dipped in the solvent that comes with the filler, then press the paste into the scratch with the putty knife. Immediately wipe away excess filler with the cloth. If the filler shrinks as it hardens, wait an hour and repeat the process.

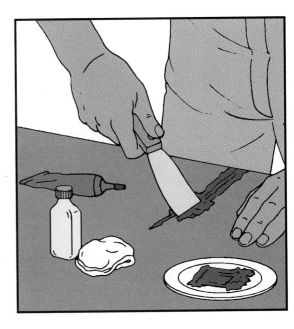

Restoring a blemished butcher block.

◆ Set the edge of a steel scraper against the butcher block at a 60° angle, beveled edge up *(left)*, and pull it across the blemished area.

◆ If scraping fails, run an orbital electric sander with medium-grit sandpaper over an area slightly larger than the stain. Keep the sander moving to avoid grinding a depression into the surface.

◆ Smooth the surface with fine-grit sandpaper, and apply vegetable oil or a nontoxic finish.

REGLUING PLASTIC LAMINATE

1. Applying the adhesive.

◆ First try reviving the old adhesive by placing a cloth over the area and heating it with a cool iron, then press the loose piece down with a roller.

◆ Alternatively, lift the loose edge gently and scrape out dried glue with a utility knife. Blow out any loose debris with a straw.

◆ Using a toothpick, spread carpenter's glue sparingly on the exposed countertop core *(right)*.

◆ Press the laminate back into place and wipe off excess glue.

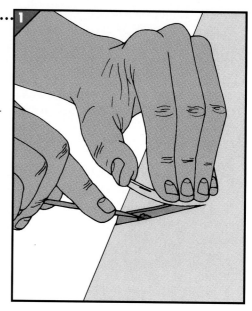

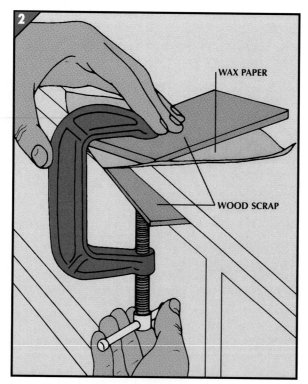

WAX PAPER

WOOD SCRAP

2. Clamping down the repair.

◆ Lay a piece of wax paper over the repair, then cover it with a scrap of wood. With another scrap protecting the underside of the countertop, clamp the repair tightly *(left)*.

◆ Wait 24 hours for the glue to set, then release the clamp.

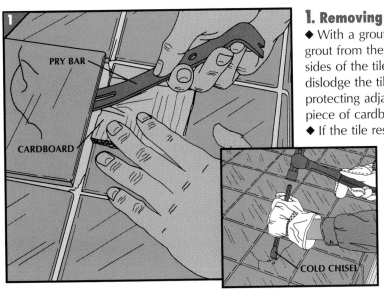

1. Removing the tile.

◆ With a grout saw, scratch the grout from the joints on all four sides of the tile, then attempt to dislodge the tile with a pry bar, protecting adjacent tiles with a piece of cardboard *(left)*.

◆ If the tile resists prying, drill four holes near the center with a masonry bit, then chip out the tile with a cold chisel and hammer *(inset)*.

◆ Scrape any old adhesive or grout from the opening in the countertop with a putty knife or a cold chisel, making the surface as even as possible. Wipe away dust with a damp cloth.

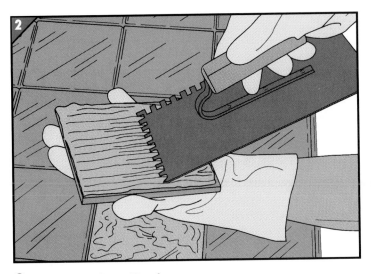

2. Applying the adhesive.

Use the flat edge of a notched trowel to coat the back of the replacement tile with adhesive, then comb the adhesive with the notched edge, leaving visible ridges *(above)*.

3. Setting the tile.

◆ Place the tile in the opening, and gently set it into place with a slight back-and-forth twisting motion.

◆ Remove any adhesive from the tile surface with a damp cloth.

◆ Lay an 18-inch length of 2-by-4 on the replacement tile. Tap the board with a hammer to bring the surface of the replacement tile even with the surfaces of the other tiles.

◆ Allow the adhesive to cure, then grout the surrounding joints with your fingertip *(inset)*.

A GLASS INSET FOR A SCARRED COUNTERTOP

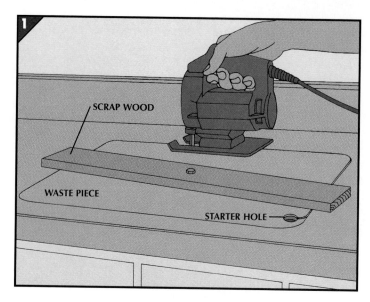

1. Cutting the hole.
◆ Set the rim of the inset or the template provided by its manufacturer over the damaged area, and mark a cut line on the countertop.
◆ Loosely bolt a piece of scrap lumber to the countertop to support the cutout as you saw *(left)*.
◆ Just inside a corner of the marked area, drill a starter hole for a saber saw. Cut out the opening, rotating the board ahead of the saw as you go.
◆ Lift out the waste piece with the board, and test-fit the metal rim in the opening. If necessary, enlarge the opening slightly with a coarse file.

SCRAP WOOD

WASTE PIECE

STARTER HOLE

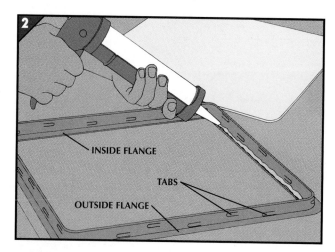

INSIDE FLANGE

TABS

OUTSIDE FLANGE

2. Preparing the inset.
◆ Set the rim of the inset upside down and squeeze a thin bead of silicone caulk around the inside flange *(left)*.
◆ Turn the glass piece upside down and press it into the rim of the inset. With a screwdriver, bend the metal tabs along the rim outward to hold the glass in place.
◆ Apply a heavier bead of caulk to the outside flange of the rim, then set the assembly into the countertop.

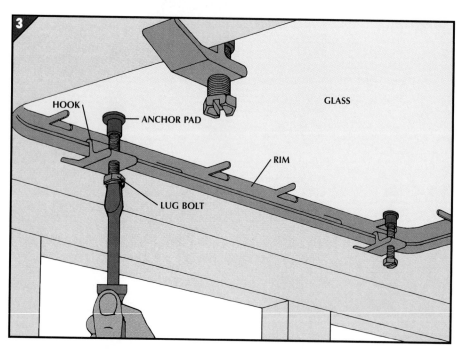

HOOK

ANCHOR PAD

GLASS

RIM

LUG BOLT

3. Fastening the inset.
◆ Underneath the countertop, hook one of the lugs provided by the manufacturer over the edge of the metal rim, insert the lug bolt and thread it into an anchor pad, then screw the pad against the underside of the inset piece *(left)*.
◆ Repeat this procedure on the lug and bolt diagonally opposite, then on the remaining bolts.
◆ On the countertop, use a putty knife to scrape off excess caulk around the edge of the rim.

AN INLAY OF CERAMIC TILES

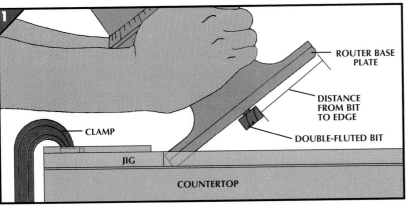

Labels: ROUTER BASE PLATE, DISTANCE FROM BIT TO EDGE, DOUBLE-FLUTED BIT, CLAMP, JIG, COUNTERTOP

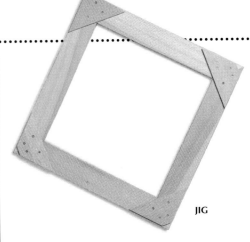

JIG

1. Measuring the area.
◆ Draw a rectangle on the countertop $\frac{1}{4}$ inch larger in each dimension than the area that is to be tiled.
◆ In each corner of the rectangle—and touching its edges—drill a $\frac{1}{4}$-inch hole to the depth of the router cut you plan.
◆ Measure between the router bit and the base plate edge. Double the measurement, and add the result to the dimensions of the rectangle. Make a jig for the router *(photograph)*, using these figures as inside dimensions.
◆ Clamp the jig in place. After adjusting the router to cut half the planned depth, place the router base against the jig *(above, left)*.

2. Routing the inset area.
◆ Turn on the router, lower it into the countertop, and move it to the center.
◆ To ensure support for the router, cut a clockwise spiral *(right)* to the edge of the jig, then rout along the perimeter. Set the bit to the full depth and retrace the spiral.
◆ Beginning in the center, finish routing the remaining countertop inside the jig.
◆ To remove small countertop remnants in corners around the drill holes, score the laminate with a laminate blade in a utility knife, then chisel away the underlying wood.

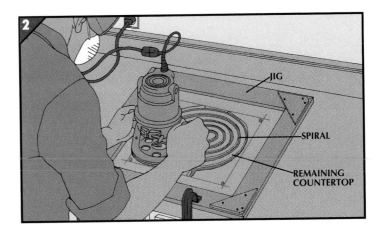

Labels: JIG, SPIRAL, REMAINING COUNTERTOP

3. Laying the tiles.
◆ Cut a piece of plywood to fit the routed area, and glue it in place.
◆ With a notched trowel, spread adhesive over the plywood. Then set the tiles in the inset *(right)*, and let the adhesive cure according to the manufacturer's recommendations.
◆ Grout and seal the joints between tiles as described on page 111.
◆ After the grout has cured, caulk the $\frac{1}{4}$-inch space between the tiles and the countertop with silicone caulk.

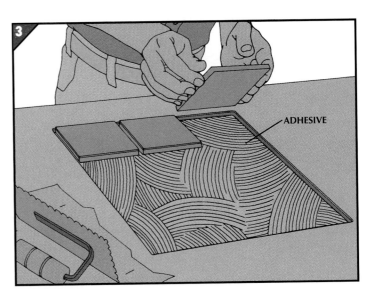

ADHESIVE

Repairing Kitchen Floors

Kitchen floors are high-traffic areas that take a beating in normal everyday use. For this reason, most are made either of durable, resilient vinyl—laid in sheets or square tiles—or of tough, rigid ceramic tile.

Rugged as they are, these materials can still be damaged by common household accidents. Dropped utensils can gouge resilient flooring or crack ceramic tile, and hot liquids can blister a vinyl surface.

Fortunately, such flaws can usually be patched, and it is not necessary to tear out the entire floor. Replacing a broken ceramic tile is described on page 17. Before under-taking any repairs on resilient flooring, read the information on asbestos on page 22.

Sometimes vinyl tiles or sections of sheet flooring work loose from the plywood underlayment to which they are bonded. This problem should be corrected immediately, before the flooring becomes damaged or kitchen spills seep through to the underlayment and subfloor.

Damaged Wall Base: Also prone to nicks and splits from accidental blows is the wall base—either quarter-round wooden lengths called shoe molding or flexible vinyl strips—which conceals the joint between the kitchen floor and the walls. Sometimes a section of undamaged wall base must be removed in order to repair the adjacent flooring. If shoe molding is removed carefully, the same piece can be remounted afterward.

Vinyl molding usually needs to be replaced, because it is not practical to try to remove the adhesive from the old piece. New molding in various widths and colors is available at any building-supply center. If you buy it in one long roll, cut it into workable lengths—4 to 6 feet—before installing it.

 **TOOLS**

Utility knife
Linoleum knife
Putty knife
Pry bar
Nail set
Heat gun
Hand roller
Notched spreader
Glue injector

 **MATERIALS**

Wood filler
Vinyl-tile adhesive
Seam sealer

SAFETY TIPS

◆ *Heat guns heat a stream of air to between about 250° and 1,100° F. The lowest temperature setting on the gun will usually suffice to soften the adhesive under kitchen flooring. Always wear thick work gloves to protect against burns.*
◆ *Wear rubber gloves when mixing, removing, or applying flooring adhesive. Open all doors and windows in the room, and avoid inhaling the fumes.*

REPLACING SHOE MOLDING

1. Loosening the molding.
◆ First, run a utility knife between the molding and the baseboard to break the paint seal.
◆ Starting at a door or an outside corner, work the blade of a wide putty knife into the seam. Gently lever the piece of molding far enough from the baseboard to allow the insertion of a pry bar into the gap.

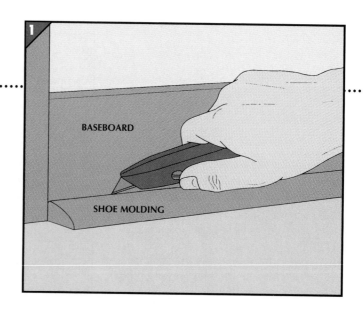

BASEBOARD

SHOE MOLDING

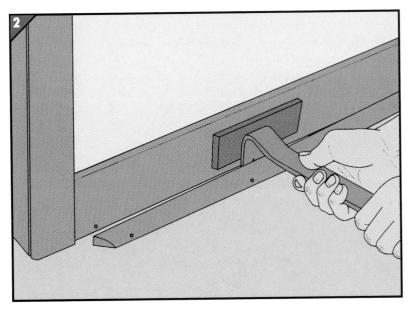

2. Removing the molding.

◆ Using a piece of wood or cardboard to protect the baseboard, work the pry bar along the molding, levering it out slightly at each nail. When the entire piece is thus loosened, return to the first nail and repeat the process. Work slowly; do not try to force the piece out all at once.

◆ If you are replacing damaged molding, save the old pieces as a guide for cutting strips of new molding.

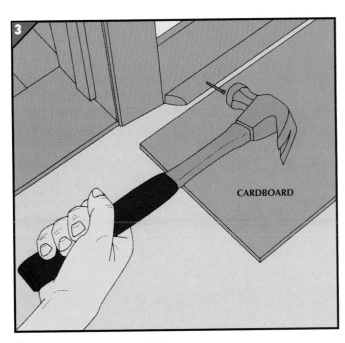

CARDBOARD

3. Installing new molding.

◆ Lay the old pieces of molding against a strip of new molding, and mark the proper lengths. Cut the new pieces with a backsaw. Use a miter box to achieve accurate 45° angles where two pieces meet at a corner.

◆ Install the new pieces in the reverse order from which you removed the old molding, ending at a door or an outside corner.

◆ Lay a piece of cardboard on the floor to protect the finish, then drive a $1\frac{1}{2}$-inch finishing nail through the center of the molding 1 inch from its end. Drive a nail every 12 inches along the length of the piece.

◆ Place a nail set against the head of each finishing nail in turn and, with a hammer, tap the nail set until the heads are below the surface of the molding.

4. Filling the holes and gaps.

◆ Use a putty knife to work wood filler into nail holes and any gaps between molding pieces.

◆ When the filler is dry, sand the wood and the filler, then finish the shoe molding with paint or stain.

BASEBOARDS OF VINYL

1. Removing the wall base.

◆ Hold the nozzle of a heat gun a few inches from the end of a section of wall base, and sweep it back and forth for about 15 seconds to soften the adhesive.

◆ Work the tip of a putty knife behind the heated wall base, and separate it from the wall. Continue moving down the length of the section with the heat gun and putty knife until the entire strip comes off.

◆ Soften any adhesive left on the wall, and scrape it off with the putty knife.

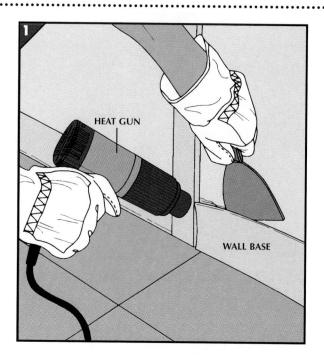

HEAT GUN

WALL BASE

2. Installing new wall base.

◆ Use a notched spreader to coat the back of the wall base evenly with adhesive to within $\frac{1}{2}$ inch of its edges.

◆ Press the section into place on the wall, making sure the bottom edge touches the floor. Where a strip must fit around a corner, warm the strip with the heat gun so that it bends easily.

◆ When the entire section is in place, run a hand roller back and forth over it several times to bond it to the wall (*above*).

⚠ CAUTION

Asbestos

If your resilient kitchen floor was installed before 1986, the flooring or the adhesive underneath may contain asbestos. When damaged, these materials can release microscopic asbestos fibers into the air, creating severe long-term health risks. Unless you know for certain that your floor does not contain asbestos, assume that it does, and follow these precautions when making any repairs:

❗ *Always wear a dual-cartridge respirator. Asbestos fibers will pass right through an ordinary dust mask.*

❗ *Never sand resilient flooring or the underlying adhesive.*

❗ *Try to remove the damaged flooring in one piece. If it looks likely to break or crumble, wet it before removal to reduce the chance of raising dust.*

❗ *When scraping off old adhesive, always use a heat gun to keep it tacky or a spray bottle to keep it wet.*

❗ *If vacuuming is necessary, rent or buy a wet/dry shop vac with a HEPA (High Efficiency Particulate Air) filtration system.*

❗ *Place the damaged flooring, adhesive, and HEPA filter in a polyethylene trash bag at least 6 millimeters thick, and seal it immediately.*

❗ *Contact your local environmental protection office for guidance as to proper disposal.*

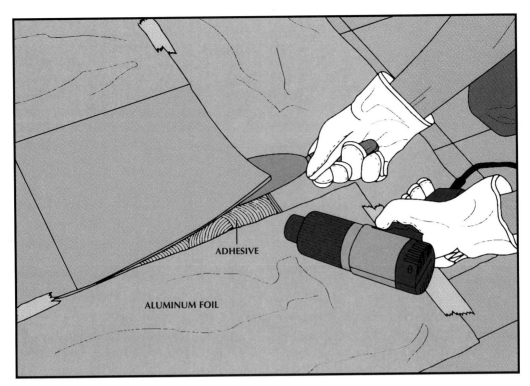

ADHESIVE

ALUMINUM FOIL

Resealing tiles.
◆ Tape sheets of aluminum foil over the adjacent tiles to protect them from being damaged by the heat gun.
◆ Lift the loose corner of the tile with a putty knife, and move the heat gun back and forth until the adhesive on the underlayment and the bottom of the tile is tacky.
◆ Press the tile down firmly, cover it with a cloth, and place several thick books or some equivalent weight on the cloth. After 30 minutes, remove the cloth and check the tile. If it lifts again, the tile must be removed and reglued.

Regluing tiles.
◆ Soften the adhesive with the heat gun while gently lifting the tile with the putty knife until it can be pulled off.
◆ Using the heat gun and putty knife, remove the old adhesive from the back of the tile and the exposed underlayment.
◆ With a notched spreader, coat the underlayment evenly with vinyl-tile adhesive, leaving visible ridges in it (*left*).
◆ Let the adhesive set according to the manufacturer's instructions, then fit the tile into the opening and press it down firmly with a hand roller.

REPLACING DAMAGED TILES

1. Removing tiles.

To remove a damaged tile that is still securely bonded to the underlayment, lay a straightedge across the tile about 1 inch from its edge to protect the adjacent tile from the heat gun. Cut through the tile along the straightedge with a linoleum knife.

◆ Sweep the nozzle of the heat gun back and forth along the slit until the adhesive is soft enough to allow the insertion of a putty knife under the edge of the tile, then work the tile loose and remove it. Remove adjacent damaged tiles the same way.

◆ If any damaged tiles were cut when installed to fit against a wall or around an obstruction, use them as templates to make matching replacement tiles.

2. Spreading the adhesive.

◆ Remove the old adhesive from the underlayment with a heat gun and putty knife.

◆ With a notched spreader, coat the underlayment with vinyl-tile adhesive, leaving ridges, and let it set according to the manufacturer's instructions.

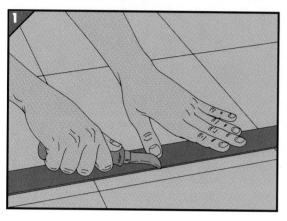

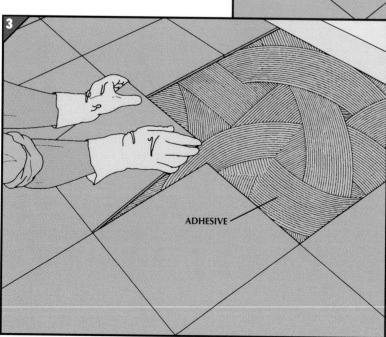

ADHESIVE

3. Installing the new tiles.

◆ Fit a replacement tile in a corner of the opening where it abuts two existing tiles.

◆ Lay whole tiles first, and finish with those that have been cut to fit.

◆ With a hand roller, firmly press down all the new tiles flush with each other and the surrounding tiles.

◆ With a damp cloth, immediately wipe up any excess adhesive. Don't walk on the replacement tiles until the adhesive has dried completely. This usually takes 24 hours.

REGLUING A LIFTED EDGE

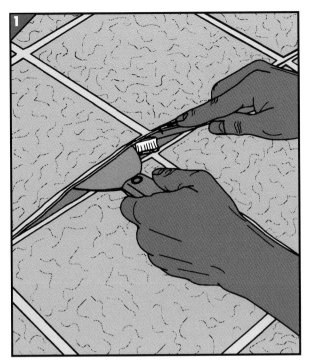

1. Removing the old adhesive.
◆ Raise the loose edge with a putty knife, then use an old toothbrush moistened with undiluted liquid floor cleaner to scrub under it.
◆ While the old adhesive is still wet, use a sharp knife to scrape it from the area along the seam.
◆ Wipe the area clean with a cloth, and let it dry.

2. Applying the adhesive.
◆ Raise the lifted edge again, and use a small putty knife to spread a thin layer of adhesive on the underlayment. Let it set for the specified time.
◆ Pressing firmly, run a hand roller along the edge to bind it to the adhesive.
◆ Immediately wipe up any excess adhesive with a damp cloth, then cover the seam with a dry cloth and place several thick books on it.

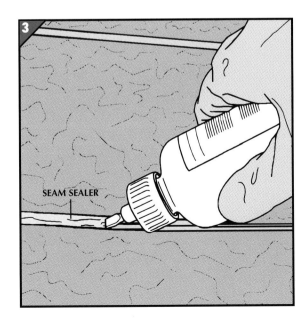

SEAM SEALER

3. Sealing the seam.
◆ Let the adhesive dry according to the manufacturer's instructions, then seal the edge using a commercial seam sealer recommended for your type of flooring.
◆ Working from one end of the edge to the other, hold the applicator at an angle and gently squeeze out a continuous bead.
◆ Keep traffic off the edge until the sealer is dry.

⚠️ **CAUTION** *Seam sealer is toxic and flammable. Follow all safety precautions on the label.*

FLATTENING A BLISTER

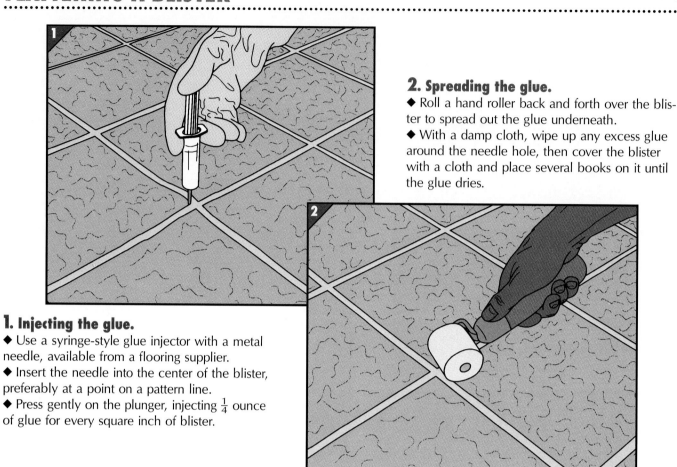

2. Spreading the glue.
◆ Roll a hand roller back and forth over the blister to spread out the glue underneath.
◆ With a damp cloth, wipe up any excess glue around the needle hole, then cover the blister with a cloth and place several books on it until the glue dries.

1. Injecting the glue.
◆ Use a syringe-style glue injector with a metal needle, available from a flooring supplier.
◆ Insert the needle into the center of the blister, preferably at a point on a pattern line.
◆ Press gently on the plunger, injecting $\frac{1}{4}$ ounce of glue for every square inch of blister.

A PATCH FOR SHEET FLOORING

1. Making a patch.
◆ Place a matching, slightly larger piece of flooring over the damaged section, and carefully align the pattern.
◆ Secure the replacement piece to the floor with masking tape.

26

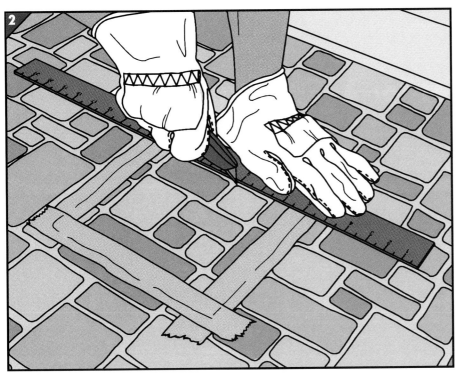

2. Cutting out the damaged section.

◆ Use a utility knife and a straightedge to cut the replacement piece and the damaged section simultaneously, following pattern lines wherever possible.
◆ Lift off the replacement piece, and dispose of the tape and cut edges.
◆ If the damaged section remains adhered to the underlayment, work the tip of the knife between the upper wear layer and the backing, and peel off the upper layer.
◆ Wet the backing with a solution of dishwashing liquid and water, and scrape it off the underlayment with a putty knife.

3. Installing the replacement section.

◆ With a notched spreader, coat the underlayment with an even layer of adhesive.
◆ Let the adhesive set according to the manufacturer's instructions, then fit the replacement piece into the hole.
◆ Press it firmly into place with a hand roller, and immediately wipe up any excess adhesive with a damp cloth.
◆ When the adhesive is dry, seal the edges of the patch with seam sealer *(page 25, Step 3)*.

2

Simple Fixes for Appliances

Major kitchen appliances are built to give many years of reliable service, but when a problem arises, it can often appear more serious than it really is. In many instances, you can make repairs easily—and safely—without specialized knowledge of the machines. Doing the work yourself not only spares you the cost of a service call, but may well save money on parts, too.

Burner Unit on a Gas Range →

How to Restore a Dishwasher to Health

The most common complaints about dishwashers—they leak, don't drain, or don't clean well—often arise from clogs or mechanical breakdowns that are easily fixed, and in some cases the dishwasher may not be at fault.

Hot Water Helps to Clean: Dirty or spotted dishes, for example, may simply be the result of insufficiently hot water. To check your water supply, place a candy thermometer or meat thermometer in a coffee mug,

then turn the kitchen tap to its hottest setting and run water into the mug for 2 minutes. If the temperature is below 120°, raise the setting on your water heater to 120°.

Fixing Those Leaks: Inspect the gaskets around the door, and check hose connections at the water inlet valve, pump, and drain valve. Reseat a slipped gasket in its track, and tighten or replace any loose hose clamps. Replace hoses that look as

if they are cracked or brittle.

More serious are problems involving the pump, motor, or timer, as these three parts are the hardest to fix. Only disassembling and cleaning the pump is shown (*page 34*)—in all other cases you should call for service.

⚠ **CAUTION** *Before attempting any repair of a dishwasher, turn off the power to the machine at the house service panel.*

TOOLS

Multitester
Slip-joint pliers
Screwdriver
Adjustable wrench

Candy thermometer or
   meat thermometer
Tweezers

Anatomy of a dishwasher.

To begin a cycle, the timer signals the water inlet valve to open, allowing water into the tub. The water mixes with detergent, is heated to about 140° by the heating element, and is pumped through the small apertures of the spray arm against the dishes to clean them. Then the dishes are rinsed and the tub drained, and the heating element turns on again to dry the dishes.

To drain the tub at the end of the wash cycle, a dishwasher will have either a drain valve or a reversible motor to pump out the water. Most models have a spray tower—a pipe that carries water to the upper spray arm, as shown here.

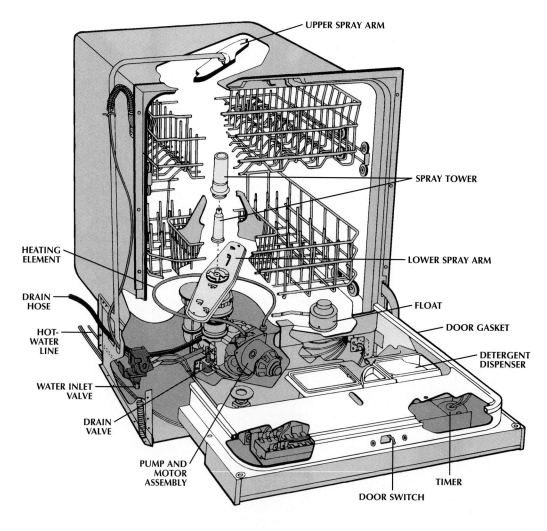

UPPER SPRAY ARM
SPRAY TOWER
LOWER SPRAY ARM
FLOAT
DOOR GASKET
DETERGENT DISPENSER
TIMER
DOOR SWITCH
PUMP AND MOTOR ASSEMBLY
DRAIN VALVE
WATER INLET VALVE
HOT-WATER LINE
DRAIN HOSE
HEATING ELEMENT

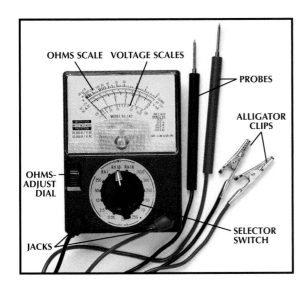

OHMS SCALE VOLTAGE SCALES

PROBES

ALLIGATOR
CLIPS

OHMS-
ADJUST
DIAL

JACKS

SELECTOR
SWITCH

The versatile multitester.

A multitester can measure the voltage and current (amperes) reaching an electrical component, as well as its resistance in ohms.

◆ Turn the selector switch to the correct value of amperes, AC volts, DC volts, or ohms you want to measure, and read the scale on the meter. Always use a setting higher than the value expected. The ohms scale is particularly useful in appliance repairs for identifying which part of the machine has failed.

◆ To calibrate the multitester for resistance measurements, select the RX1 (resistance times 1) scale and touch the probes together. Turn the ohms-adjust dial until the meter reads 0 ohms. For other tests, follow the directions in the owner's manual.

Troubleshooting Guide

PROBLEM	REMEDY
Dishes dirty or spotted.	Test water temperature. Check for binding or broken parts in detergent dispenser. Look for obstructions, such as utensils, that fall and block spray arm. Check and clean spray arm *(page 32)*. Check and clean pump *(page 34)*; replace impellers if corroded or chipped. Check and clean filter screen, if there is one *(page 32)*.
Dishwasher doesn't fill with water.	Test water inlet valve solenoid and inspect filter screen *(page 33)*. Check for obstruction propping up float; test float switch *(page 33)*. Check door latch; test door switch *(page 32)*. Check and clean filter screen, if there is one *(page 32)*.
Dishwasher drains during fill.	Inspect drain valve; test valve solenoid and replace it if necessary *(page 34)*.
Water doesn't shut off.	Remove any debris on underside of float; test float switch *(page 33)*. Test water inlet valve *(page 33)*.
Motor doesn't run.	Check for blown fuse or tripped circuit breaker. Adjust door latch if necessary; test door switch *(page 32)*.
Motor hums but doesn't run.	Check and clean pump *(page 34)*; if it still doesn't work, call for service.
Poor water drainage.	Check for clogged air gap *(page 32)*. Check the drain hose for kinks and clogs; remove any that you find. Check and clean filter screen, if there is one *(page 32)*. Check for clogged drain valve and test drain valve solenoid *(page 34)*. Check and clean pump *(page 34)*; replace impellers if corroded or chipped.
Dishwasher leaks around door.	Adjust door latch so door closes tightly *(page 32)*. Replace door gasket if the rubber is hardened or damaged.
Dishwasher leaks from bottom or below door.	Seal any cracks in tub with silicone rubber sealant or epoxy glue. Tighten water inlet valve connection. Look for loose pump seals or heating element nuts. Check spray arm, especially bottom of arm, for holes.
Door is difficult to close.	Adjust or oil door catch *(page 32)*. Replace catch if broken.

Opening a clogged air gap.

◆ Find the air gap on the back rim of the sink between the dishwasher and the sink faucet. Pull off the chrome cover, and unscrew the plastic cap.

◆ With tweezers, remove any debris from the small tube in the center of the air gap *(right)*.

◆ Clean the cover and cap if necessary; screw on the cap and snap the cover in place.

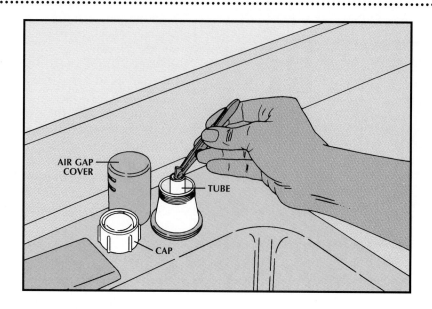

AIR GAP COVER

TUBE

CAP

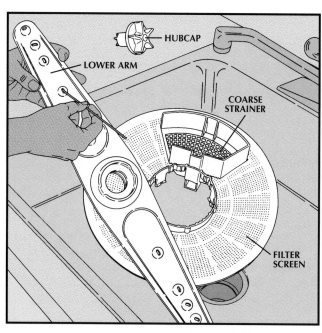

HUBCAP

LOWER ARM

COARSE STRAINER

FILTER SCREEN

Cleaning the spray arm and filter screen.

◆ After sliding out the lower dish rack, twist off the plastic hubcap, if there is one, that holds the lower spray arm in place, and lift off the arm.

◆ If your machine has a removable coarse strainer and filter screen, unsnap and remove them; otherwise, clean them in place.

◆ Clean out the slotted holes in the spray arm with a wire. Scrub the strainer and filter screen with a stiff brush, and then rinse all three before reinstalling them.

◆ Unclog the holes in the upper spray arm without removing the arm from its holder.

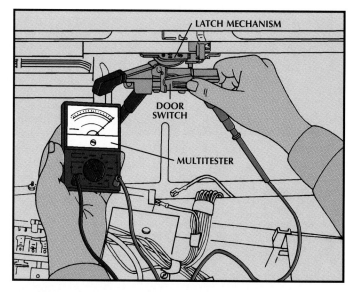

LATCH MECHANISM

DOOR SWITCH

MULTITESTER

Checking the door latch and switch.

◆ If the latch is difficult to close, lubricate the mechanism with light machine oil. On many models, the latch can be adjusted for a better fit by loosening the mounting screws, sliding the latch in or out, then retightening the screws.

◆ To test the door switch *(above)*, remove the screws on the inside of the door that secure the control panel. Close and lock the door. Gently pull off the panel and disconnect the wires from the door switch terminals, behind the latch. Attach multitester clips to the terminals, and check switch resistance *(page 31)*; any reading other than 0 ohms indicates a faulty switch.

◆ Replace the switch by removing its retaining screws, installing a new switch, and reconnecting the wires.

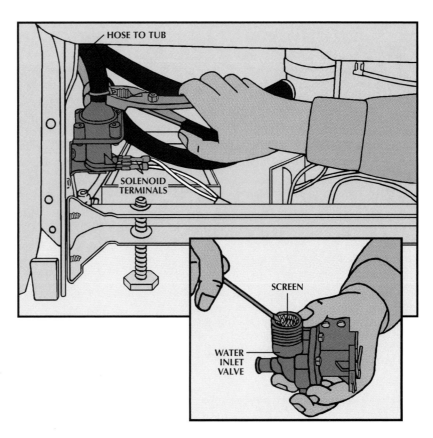

Servicing the water inlet valve.

◆ Turn off the power and water supply to the dishwasher.

◆ With a shallow pan handy, use slip-joint pliers to remove the hose that connects the inlet valve to the tub *(right)*. Then disconnect the flexible copper hot-water line with an adjustable wrench.

◆ Unscrew the valve from its mounting bracket. Without removing the filter screen, scrape it clean *(inset)* and rinse. If the valve appears cracked or otherwise damaged, replace it.

◆ With the multitester, check the solenoid. You should get a reading of between 60 and 500 ohms. Replace the valve assembly if the solenoid is faulty.

◆ Reinstall the valve, then reattach the hot-water line and hose, and tighten all connections.

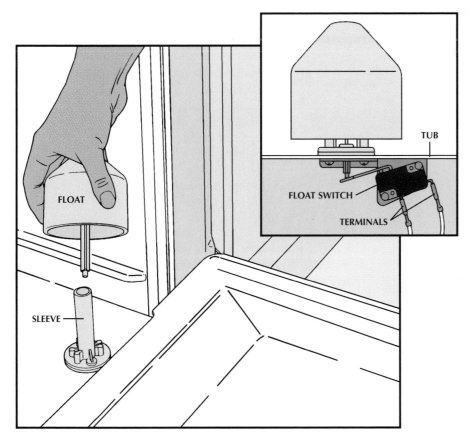

Cleaning and testing the float and its switch.

◆ Lift the float out of its sleeve, and remove any debris from the bottom of the float. Clean out the sleeve as well.

◆ Slide the float into the sleeve and run the dishwasher. If no water enters the machine or if it overflows, turn off the power to the dishwasher at the main service panel, bail out any water in the tub, and remove the access panel below the door.

◆ Test the float switch *(inset)* located under the tub by touching the multitester probes to the terminals. You should get 0 ohms with the switch on *(float down)* and infinity with the switch off *(float up)*.

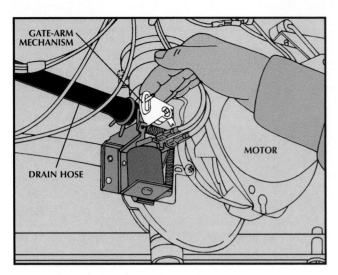

GATE-ARM MECHANISM

DRAIN HOSE

MOTOR

Inspecting the drain valve assembly.

Remove the panel below the door and count the number of wires attached to the motor. Two or three wires indicates a nonreversible motor; four or more is reversible. Only nonreversible motors have drain valves. Locate the valve and its gate-arm mechanism. Move the arm by hand *(above)*; if it doesn't move freely up and down on its two springs, replace them.

Testing the drain valve solenoid.

Disconnect the wires from the drain valve solenoid terminals and check resistance. If you do not get a reading between 60 and 500 ohms, replace the solenoid.

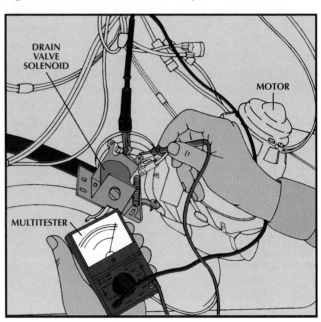

DRAIN VALVE SOLENOID

MOTOR

MULTITESTER

CLEANING THE PUMP

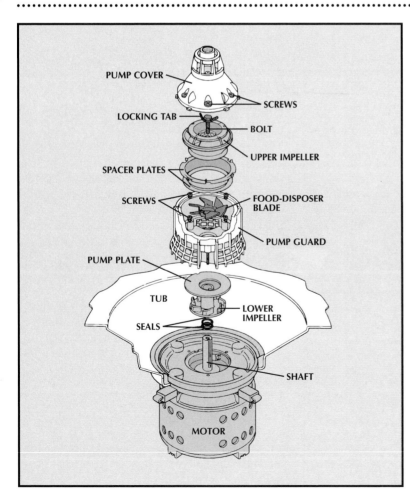

PUMP COVER

SCREWS

LOCKING TAB

BOLT

UPPER IMPELLER

SPACER PLATES

SCREWS

FOOD-DISPOSER BLADE

PUMP GUARD

PUMP PLATE

TUB

LOWER IMPELLER

SEALS

SHAFT

MOTOR

Getting to the impellers.

◆ Take off the lower spray arm *(page 32)*, then remove all screws from the pump cover, exposing the upper impeller.

◆ If there is a bolt-locking tab, bend it up to clear the bolt, then unscrew the bolt, freeing the upper impeller. Check the impeller for debris and for worn or broken blades; clean or replace it as necessary.

◆ Lift out the spacer plates and the food-disposer blade under the impeller; clean the blade.

◆ To reach the lower impeller, unfasten the screws holding the pump guard and remove it. Pull off the pump plate and clean the impeller.

◆ If the lower impeller is damaged, pry it off the motor shaft with a screwdriver or remove it with a pair of locking pliers. When installing a new impeller, replace the underlying seals before pushing the impeller onto the shaft. If the impeller will not slide on easily, sand any rust off the shaft to make it smoother.

◆ To reassemble the pump, first replace the pump plate and screw on the pump guard. Attach the food-disposer blade and spacer plates, then the upper impeller. Secure with the bolt, and put the locking tab, if there is one, on top of the bolt. Screw on the pump cover, and replace the spray arm.

Dealing with a Stuck Garbage Disposer

When a disposer stops working, it is usually because the grinding mechanism has jammed. Bits of food, glass, metal, plastic, or rubber can get caught between the spinning flywheel and the stationary grind ring, causing the motor to overheat and cut off. This may also happen if you pack the unit too tightly. Before starting to work on the disposer, check for a blown fuse or for a tripped circuit breaker at the main electrical panel.

If the suggestions below don't fix the problem, the disposer should be replaced because repairs will probably cost as much as a new unit. Check your warranty; most run from 3 to 7 years and cover repairs or replacement.

⚠️ **CAUTION** *Always turn off the power at the main panel or unplug the disposer—if it is an outlet unit—before reaching into it.*

Resetting the motor.

If the motor doesn't hum at all, reach into the disposer and feel around for any objects that may be jamming it. Let the motor cool down for 15 minutes, then switch on the power at the main panel and gently push the reset button on the bottom of the unit until you hear it click *(below)*.

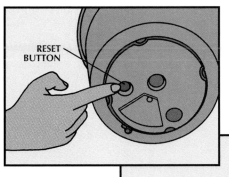

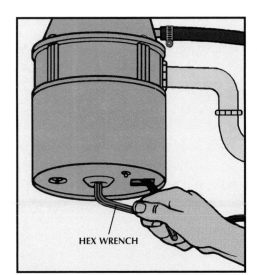

Freeing the grind ring.

If the motor hums but the disposer doesn't grind, take a $\frac{1}{4}$-inch hex wrench (or the wrench that came with the disposer) and insert one end into the hole on the bottom of the disposer *(left)*. Turn the wrench back and forth to rotate the motor shaft until it moves freely.

Unjamming the works with a broom handle.

If you are unable to clear the jam by using a hex wrench, stick a broom handle into the disposer and wedge it against one of the impeller blades on the flywheel *(left)*. Apply force until the wheel begins to turn freely, then work the wheel back and forth until it moves easily in both directions.

When a microwave oven begins to cook erratically, the fault may lie with one of several easy-to-service components within the machine. If it stops working altogether, first check that the cord has not become unplugged and that the circuit breaker has not tripped.

Defective Door Switches: The parts that fail most often are door-interlock switches. A faulty one can keep the oven from turning on and cause it to turn off unexpectedly.

As many as five switches may be present, one behind each door latch and others positioned around the door perimeter. Test each one in turn as shown on page 38.

Other Culprits: If a door switch is not to blame—and the oven light stays off when the door is open— check for a blown fuse inside the appliance. Next test the diode; diagnosis of electronic control panels is best left to a professional. However, if your oven has a dial timer and a mechanical start button, you can test two additional switches where problems originate *(page 39)*.

⚠️ **CAUTION** *An interior component called a capacitor stores an electric charge that can deliver a strong shock. Discharge the capacitor before any test or repair. The procedure* (right) *can produce a large spark.*

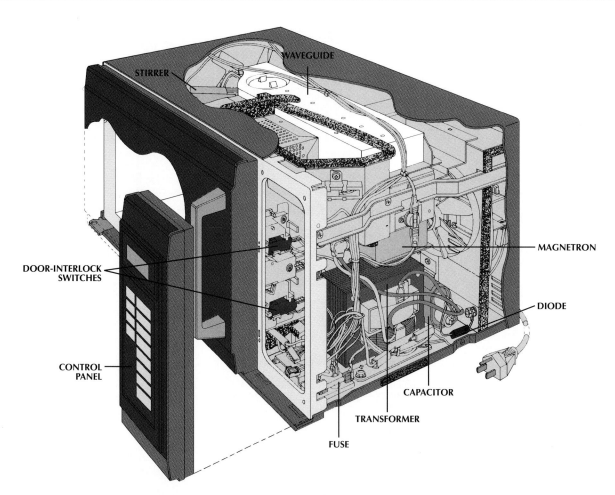

Anatomy of a microwave oven.
The heart of a microwave oven is a magnetron, which produces microwaves that travel through a waveguide into the oven. A stirrer bounces the waves around the cooking chamber, where they heat the food. Supplying the magnetron with power are a transformer, a capacitor, and a diode. These components boost 120-volt alternating-current household service to direct current (the kind provided by a battery) at 4,000 volts. A control panel on the front of the oven provides for the selection of cooking times and cycles. Safety devices include door-interlock switches, which prevent the unit from starting with the door ajar, thus prohibiting harmful microwaves from escaping, and a fuse that protects the unit from power surges.

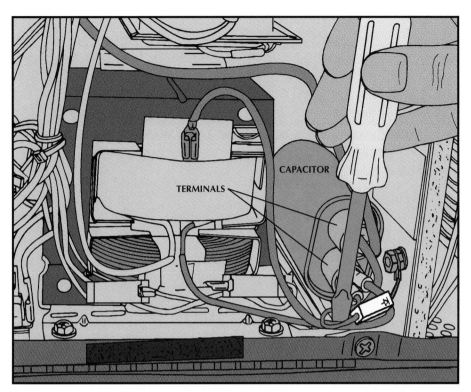

Removing the cover and discharging the capacitor.

◆ Unplug the oven, then remove the screws that secure the cover. Set the cover aside.

◆ Hold an insulated screwdriver by the handle, and lay the shaft across the metal sleeves on the capacitor's two terminals *(left)*.

◆ If this produces a spark, touch the screwdriver to the terminals again to completely discharge the capacitor. If this procedure produces no spark, the capacitor has already discharged.

UNIVERSAL MICROWAVE REPAIRS

Checking the fuse.

◆ With the oven unplugged and the cover off, locate the fuse, usually a cartridge fuse.

◆ Pull the fuse from its holder with your fingers or with a fuse puller if your fingers can't dislodge it *(right)*.

◆ To test the fuse for resistance *(page 31)*, touch a probe of a multitester to each end of the fuse.

◆ If the tester reads infinite ohms, the fuse is blown; replace it with a fuse of equal amperage.

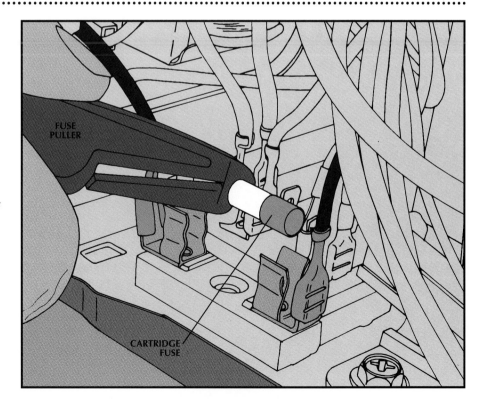

Replacing a diode.

◆ Locate the diode, which is connected to the capacitor and to the frame of the cabinet.

◆ Disconnect the diode from the capacitor and the cabinet *(right)* and examine it. Replace a diode that is cracked or burned.

◆ If there is no visible damage, set a multitester to RX1K and calibrate it *(page 31).* Touch a probe to the end of each wire *(inset),* and note the multitester reading. Then reverse the probes and check the reading again. One reading should indicate a resistance of several thousand ohms, the other infinite ohms. If the diode fails the test, replace it.

◆ Connect the new diode as the old one was connected. If the wires end in identical fittings, attach the one nearer the diode symbol to the cabinet.

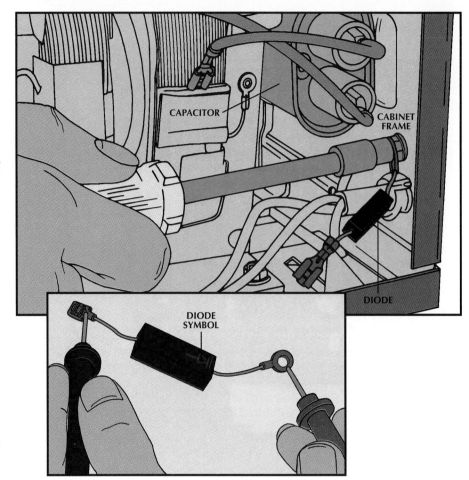

Testing a door switch.

◆ With a two-terminal switch, remove the wire from one of the terminals and check the switch for resistance *(left),* first with the door open (infinite ohms), then with it closed (0 ohms). Replace the switch if it fails either test.

◆ If a door switch has three terminals *(inset),* detach all three wires, then touch one probe to the COMMON terminal and one to the OPEN or NO terminal. A working switch will register 0 ohms with the door closed, infinite ohms with it open.

◆ Next, check for resistance between the COMMON terminal and the CLOSED or NC terminal with the door both open (0 ohms) and closed (infinite ohms). If the switch fails either test, replace it.

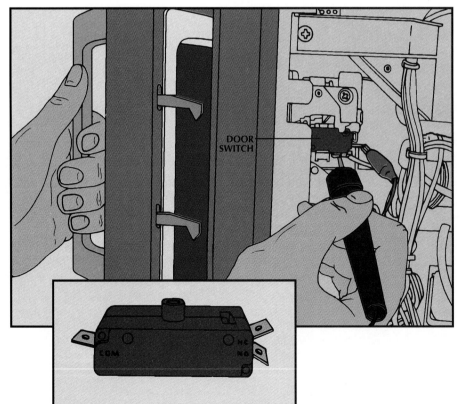

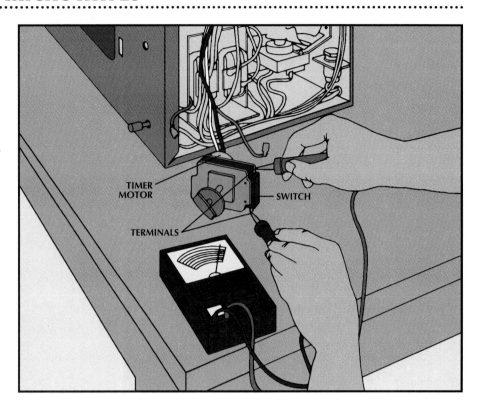

Identifying a faulty timer switch.

◆ Unscrew the timer assembly from the inside front panel and detach the wires from the two switch terminals, located on the back of the timer next to its motor.

◆ Set a multitester to RX1, set the timer for at least 1 minute, then touch the tester probes to the switch terminals *(right)*. Replace the switch if the meter registers more than 0 ohms.

On some ovens the timer switch is integrated with the timer and cannot be bought separately. Replace the entire timer assembly.

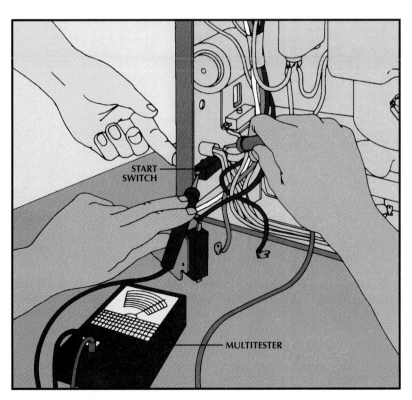

Testing the start switch.

◆ Disconnect the wires from the terminals on the switch behind the start button.

◆ Touch multitester probes to the switch terminals. There should be resistance of infinite ohms.

◆ Have a helper push the button; the meter should read 0 ohms while the button is depressed *(left)*.

◆ If the switch fails either test, replace it by unscrewing or unclipping it from the timer assembly. Install a new one, and connect the wires to its terminals.

When an Electric Range Fails to Heat

You can often locate the source of trouble on an electric range just by looking. Visible burns, pits, or cracks make it easy to identify faulty parts. If no damage is noticeable, continue your diagnosis with a multitester as shown on the following pages.

Checking the Voltage: The heating elements on an electric range run on a 240-volt circuit. High-rise buildings, however, often have three-phase 208-volt current, in which case normal readings on the multitester will be in the range of 197 to 210 volts.

Holding the Right Temperature: One common complaint about electric ranges is that the oven temperature does not match the reading on the control. A frayed or torn door gasket could be the cause, and the thermostat is also a likely culprit. To test the thermostat, place an oven thermometer in the center of the oven and set the thermostat to 350°. Let the oven heat up, then check the thermometer every 10 to 15 minutes for the next half-hour. If the temperature is within 50° of 350°, calibrate the thermostat *(page 44)*; for digital ranges, adjust the temperature at the control panel. If the temperature is more than 50° off, replace the thermostat *(page 45)*.

⚠ **CAUTION** *Before starting repairs, unplug the range or cut the power at the main service panel, then test the terminal block for incoming voltage (page 41).*

Anatomy of an electric range.

When you turn on a surface unit or the oven, current flows through a calibrated control to a heating element. The element provides resistance to the current, and the energy created radiates outward as heat.

In the oven, a rodlike capillary tube attached to the wall senses the temperature and relays the information to the thermostat, which cycles the current on or off to keep the temperature even. Digital ranges have an electronic temperature sensor.

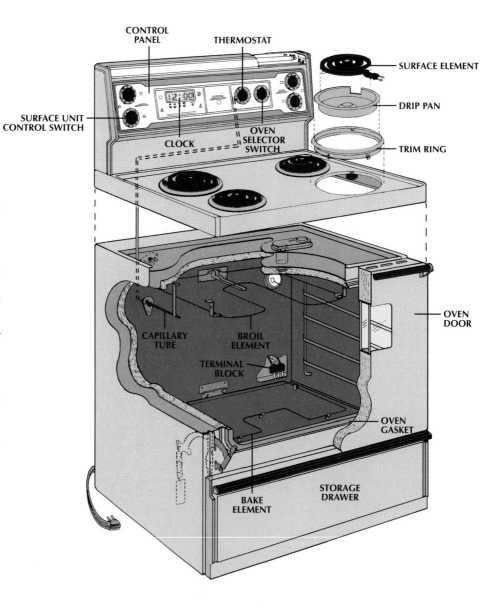

CONTROL PANEL · THERMOSTAT · SURFACE ELEMENT · DRIP PAN · TRIM RING · SURFACE UNIT CONTROL SWITCH · CLOCK · OVEN SELECTOR SWITCH · OVEN DOOR · CAPILLARY TUBE · BROIL ELEMENT · TERMINAL BLOCK · OVEN GASKET · BAKE ELEMENT · STORAGE DRAWER

Troubleshooting Guide

PROBLEM	REMEDY
Nothing works; the elements do not heat, or heat only partially.	Check fuses and circuit breakers at the main service panel. Test terminal block and replace if necessary *(page 41).*
Surface element doesn't heat.	Test element for resistance and for short; replace if necessary *(page 42).* Check connection at receptacle, and visually inspect the receptacle *(page 42).* Test the voltage at the receptacle and, if necessary, at the control switch *(page 43).* Replace the receptacle if it is faulty.
Oven doesn't heat.	Check the oven element and power to the element *(page 44).* Test thermostat for resistance; replace if necessary *(page 45).*
Oven temperature is not the same as temperature setting on control.	Test oven temperature and calibrate thermostat *(page 44).* On digital ranges, calibrate at control pad, then test the temperature sensor *(page 44).* Inspect the door gasket and replace if it is frayed or torn. Adjust oven door by loosening screws that secure inner door panel to outer door. Twist door to fit snugly, and tighten screws.
Self-cleaning oven doesn't clean.	Test the bake and broil elements *(page 44).* Test thermostat for resistance; replace if necessary *(page 45).*
Oven door doesn't close properly.	Adjust oven door *(see above).* Adjust or replace door springs.

RESTORING THE INCOMING POWER

Testing the terminal block.
◆ With the power off, pull the range out and remove the back panel.
◆ Set a multitester *(page 31)* for 250 volts and clip the leads to the block's line terminals—marked L_1 and L_2 *(right).* Restore power. If the meter doesn't show 230 to 240 volts, check for a blown fuse or tripped circuit breaker at the main service panel.
◆ Shut off the power and move a probe to the ground-wire terminal on the lower center screw. Restore power; the meter should now read 120 volts. If it does not, there may be something wrong with the house wiring; call an electrician.
◆ If the block appears burned, replace it by removing the wires and unscrewing it from the range.

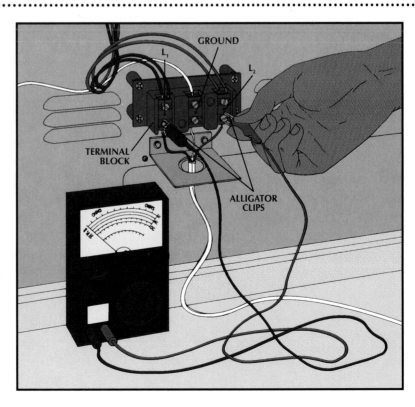

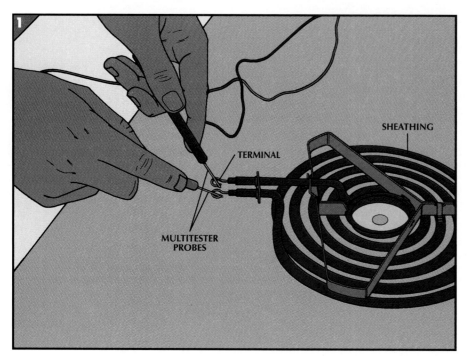

1. Testing the element.

◆ Detach the faulty element from its receptacle and inspect the coil terminals. If they are burned or pitted, replace the element and the receptacle.

◆ To test the element for resistance *(page 31),* set a multitester to RX1 and touch the probes to the terminals *(left).* The meter should read below 60 ohms. If it doesn't, the element should be replaced.

◆ If the element shows the correct resistance, check for a short circuit by leaving one probe on a terminal and placing the other probe on the sheathing. A reading of 0 ohms indicates a short; replace the element.

2. Inspecting the receptacle.

◆ Unscrew the receptacle and pull it out. Check for visible damage to the terminal blades inside the slots and for loose or damaged wires leading into the receptacle. If you find any of these, replace the receptacle.

◆ Cut the wire leading into the old receptacle as close as possible to the back of the receptacle. Strip $\frac{1}{2}$ inch of bare lead with wire strippers and splice it to the short length of wire attached to the new receptacle. Twist a wire cap over the bare ends.

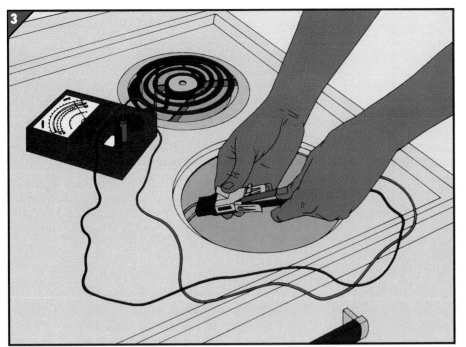

3. Checking the voltage at the receptacle.

◆ With the power off, insert a multi-tester probe into each receptacle slot so that the probe touches the terminal blade *(left)*.

◆ Set the multitester for 250 volts, restore power to the range, and turn the control knob to HIGH. If the meter does not read 230 to 240 volts, check the control switch *(Step 4)*. If the control switch is fine, replace the receptacle *(Step 2)*.

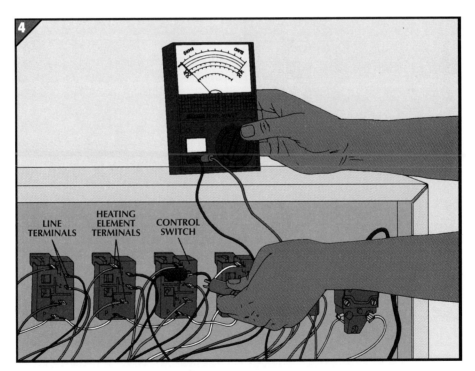

4. Testing the control switch.

◆ Locate the switch behind the rear top panel. Cut the power and put multitester clips on the switch's line terminals, marked L_1 and L_2 *(above)*. Set the multitester for 250 volts and restore power; you should get 230 to 240 volts. Turn off the power and move the clips to the heating element terminals, marked H_1 and H_2. Restore power and turn the knob to HIGH. The meter should again read 230 to 240 volts.

◆ If you only get power at L_1 and L_2, or any terminals appear burned, replace the switch. No power at L_1 and L_2 indicates loose or burned terminal block connections; tighten the wires, or replace the block *(page 41)*. If H_1 and H_2 have power but the receptacle does not, splice new range wire—available at appliance-repair shops or electronics stores—between them.

ADJUSTING AN OVEN TEMPERATURE CONTROL

Calibrating the thermostat.

◆ Pull off the thermostat knob and loosen the setscrews on the back *(near right)*. Turn the disk slightly to recalibrate the thermostat—here, moving the disk pointer one notch for each 25°. Retighten the setscrews.

◆ Some ranges have a calibration screw instead. Pull off the thermostat knob and locate the screw inside or beside the shaft *(far right)*. Adjustments vary; consult your owner's manual for which way and how far to turn the screw.

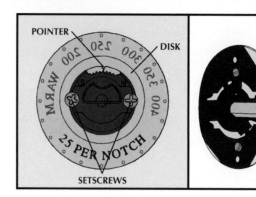

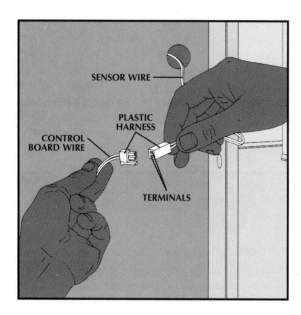

Testing digital oven controls.

◆ To test the temperature sensor—a rod inside the over on the rear wall—for resistance, pull out the range and remove the back panel. Unclip the plastic harness *(left),* and touch multitester probes to the terminals inside the harness. Check the owner's manual for the proper resistance reading.

◆ To replace a faulty sensor, unscrew the retaining plate, and pull out the sensor; then insert the new one and re-attach the plate. Connect the harness and replace the back panel.

◆ If you get the proper reading, the electronic control board is defective; call for service.

GETTING HEAT FROM A BALKY OVEN

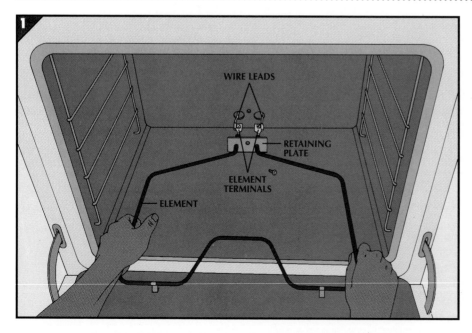

1. Examining the bake or broil element.

◆ Unscrew the element's retaining plate from the rear wall. Pull the element out and unplug the leads from their terminals or loosen the screws and disconnect the wires.

◆ Replace the element if it has burns and cracks. Cut off a burned or pitted terminal, strip about $\frac{1}{2}$ inch of its wire lead, and attach a new one.

◆ Touch multitester probes to the element terminals to check resistance. You should get 10 to 60 ohms; if you do not, replace the element.

◆ Leave one probe on a terminal and touch one to the element. A 0-ohms reading means the element is shorted; replace it.

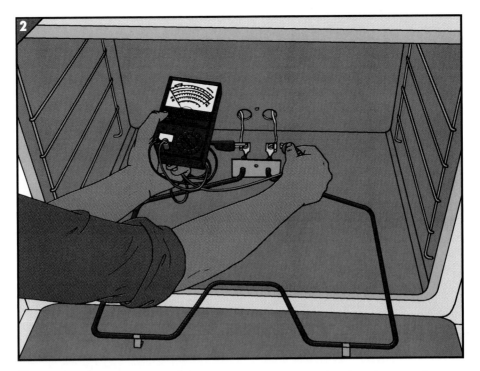

2. Testing for power to the element.

◆ Reconnect the leads and attach the multitester clips to the terminals or, if your range has them, to the screws in the element terminals *(above)*.

◆ Set the multitester for 250 volts, then restore power to the range and turn the oven to 300°. If the meter registers 230 to 240 volts after about a minute, power is reaching the element, so the element must be faulty. Turn off the power and replace the element.

◆ If the multitester does not show the proper voltage, turn off the power and check for loose wires at the oven selector switch and thermostat behind the back panel of the range.

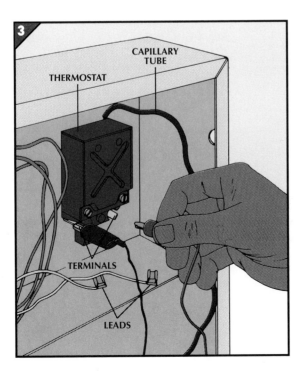

3. Checking the thermostat.

◆ Turn off the power, remove the leads from the back of the thermostat, and attach multitester clips to the terminals *(left)* to test for resistance. With the knob turned to 300° and the power off, the meter should read 0 ohms; if it does not, replace the thermostat.

◆ Examine the capillary tube; if it is damaged, replace the whole thermostat.

◆ To replace a thermostat, shut off the power, remove the leads, and unscrew the thermostat from the back panel. Unclip the capillary tube from the oven wall and pull it out from the back. Push a new tube into the oven, clip it on, and screw on the new thermostat. Reattach the leads.

45

Safe Repairs for a Gas Range

A gas range is, in essence, a network of pipes that carry gas to burners on the cooktop and in the oven, where it is mixed with air and ignited to produce a controlled flame.

Lighting the Gas: Some ranges have a high-voltage ignition module on the back panel of the range that sends current to an electric igniter when the burner is turned on. Other types use pilots that produce small, constantly burning flames that ignite the gas. Most problems with either system are caused by accumulated dirt and grease, which can foul the electrodes of electric igniters or clog the small apertures of the pilots.

Routine Maintenance: Keeping the cooking surfaces clean is the best way to avoid problems, and modern ranges are designed with this in mind. Burner grates and drip pans lift off, and the hinged cooktop can be propped open. Oven doors slide off, and both the oven bottom and the oven burner baffle are removable for easy cleaning and access to the oven burner.

⚠️ **CAUTION** *If the pilot has been out for some time or if you detect an odor of gas, ventilate the room before relighting.*

Anatomy of a gas range.

Natural gas enters the range through the supply pipe in the back. Inside, the pipe branches to carry gas to the oven burner and the manifold, which runs across the front of the range beneath the cooktop and distributes gas to the four surface burner units. An air shutter on each burner's pipe mixes air with the natural gas.

Turning the burner-control knob on the front of the range opens a valve that lets the air/gas mixture flow into the burner tube and the flash tube—where it is ignited—and then through the small holes in the burner head. The oven burner is governed by a thermostat, which senses the temperature inside the oven by means of a capillary tube.

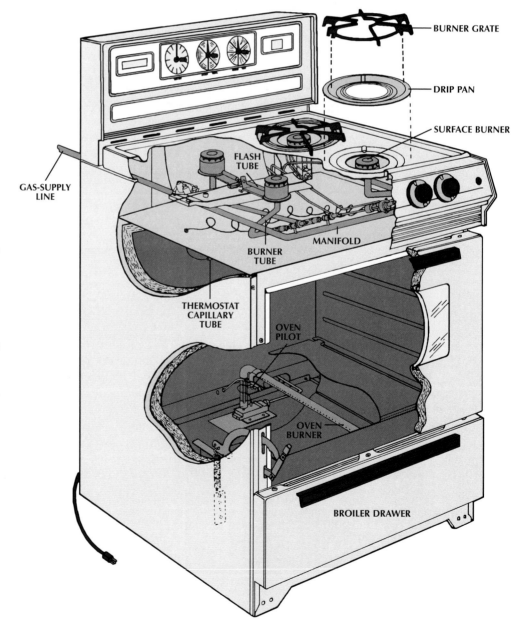

BURNER GRATE

DRIP PAN

SURFACE BURNER

FLASH TUBE

GAS-SUPPLY LINE

MANIFOLD

BURNER TUBE

THERMOSTAT CAPILLARY TUBE

OVEN PILOT

OVEN BURNER

BROILER DRAWER

Troubleshooting Guide

PROBLEM	REMEDY
Gas odor.	Ventilate the room.
	Turn burner controls to OFF.
	Check burner and oven pilots. Relight them with a match if necessary.
	If the gas odor persists, turn off gas to the range and call the gas company.
Burner won't light.	Relight extinguished pilot flames *(page 48)* or clean igniter electrodes.
	Clear the burner portholes with a thin needle *(page 48)*.
	Close the air shutter slightly *(page 48)*.
	Reposition a surface burner to align its flash tube with the pilot flame or igniter *(page 48)*.
	For ovens, check the flame switch *(page 49)*.
Pilot flame won't stay lit.	Clear the pilot opening with a thin needle *(page 48)*.
	Adjust the pilot flame *(page 48)*.
Electric igniter won't spark.	Check incoming power to the range.
	Clean igniter electrodes with a cotton swab or cloth.
	If the igniter still doesn't spark, the igniter, the wiring, or the ignition module is faulty; call for service.

The ideal flame.
In the upper photograph at right, a properly adjusted burner shows a steady, quiet flame with sharply defined blue cones about $\frac{1}{2}$ to $\frac{3}{4}$ inch high. Insufficient air reaching the burner produces a weak red or yellow flame *(below)* that may leave soot deposits on pots and pans. In the lower photograph at right, the burner is getting too much air, resulting in an uneven, noisy flame.

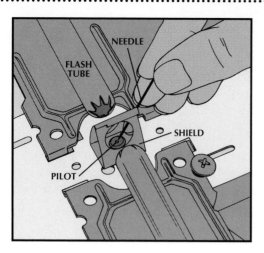

Cleaning the pilot opening.
◆ Insert a needle into the hole in the center of the pilot and move it up and down, taking care not to enlarge or deform the opening. If the metal shield over the pilot presents an obstacle, gently lift it out of the way.
◆ With all burner controls turned to the off position, relight the pilot frame with a match held at the opening.

Clearing the portholes.
◆ With the range top propped open, lift out the burner assembly. It is usually unanchored, held in place by its own weight.
◆ Push a needle through each porthole (some burners have a vertical slot instead of portholes), then wash the burner head in warm, soapy water.
◆ To reinstall the burner, slip the burner tube onto the gas manifold and align the flash tube with the pilot.

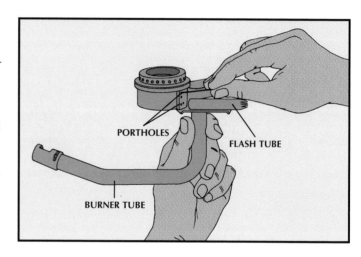

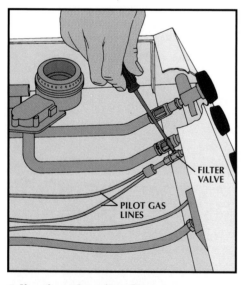

Adjusting the pilot flame.
◆ Follow the thin pilot gas lines to the filter valve at the front of the stove.
◆ Find the screw on the side of the valve, and turn it with a screwdriver until the pilot flame is a compact blue cone with little or no yellow at the tip.

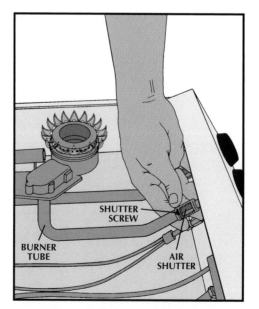

Regulating the burner flame.
◆ To adjust the airflow to a burner, first turn off all the burner controls. Locate the air shutter on the burner tube near the front of the stove.
◆ Loosen the shutter screw until the shutter either twists or slides freely, then turn the burner on high.
◆ Adjust the shutter by hand until the burner has the correct airflow (page 47) and retighten the shutter screw.

Exposing the pilot and burner.

Loosen any tabs or screws holding the oven floor in place, and lift it from the oven. Below the floor is the burner baffle *(inset),* often held in place by wing nuts. Remove them and the baffle, then pull the broiler drawer out of its opening and set it aside.

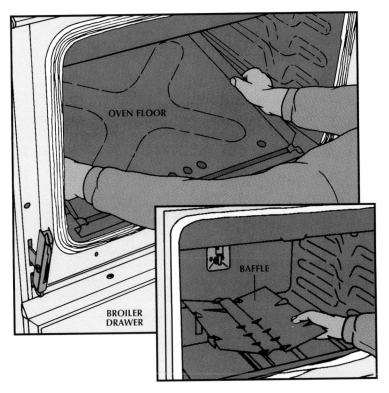

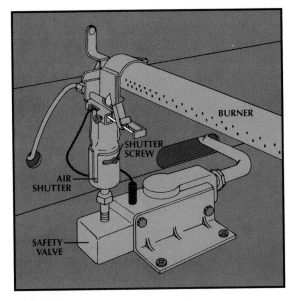

Adjusting pilot and burner flames.

◆ Relight the pilot if it has gone out. If not, increase its height. Pull the oven thermostat knob from its shaft to reveal an adjustment screw labeled "constant pilot," and turn it clockwise.

◆ Replace the knob and turn on the oven. If the burner still does not light, the thermostat or safety valve must be replaced. Call a repair service.

◆ To adjust the burner flame, turn off the oven and loosen the air-shutter screw. Change the shutter opening, then remove your hand from the oven and turn on the oven to observe the flame *(page 47).*

◆ Make additional adjustments as needed, each time turning off the burner before reaching into the oven.

◆ When the flame is satisfactory, turn off the oven, tighten the shutter screw, and replace the baffle and oven floor.

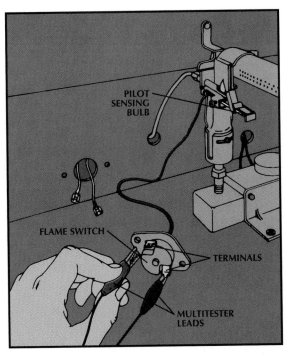

Testing the oven flame switch.

◆ Turn off electrical power to the range, check that the pilot flame is burning, then unscrew the switch from the rear oven wall.

◆ Detach the wires from the two terminals on the back of the flame switch. Check for resistance between the flame switch terminals with a multitester set at RX1 *(page 31).* A reading of 0 ohms indicates a properly working switch; call a repair service, and expect to have the oven thermostat replaced.

◆ If the multitester shows high resistance, replace the flame switch. Remove it by gently working the pilot sensing bulb from its bracket. To install a new switch, attach the wires to its terminals, screw it to the oven wall, and slip the sensing bulb into the bracket.

Two Kinds of Range Hood Ventilators

Many ranges, electric and gas, are topped by a venting range hood. The hood will contain either a fan or "squirrel-cage" blower impellers that draw smoke and grease through an aluminum mesh filter and out an exhaust duct.

To keep grease from building up around the motor and on the fan blades or on the blower impellers, wash the filter regularly in hot, soapy water or in the dishwasher, and replace it annually.

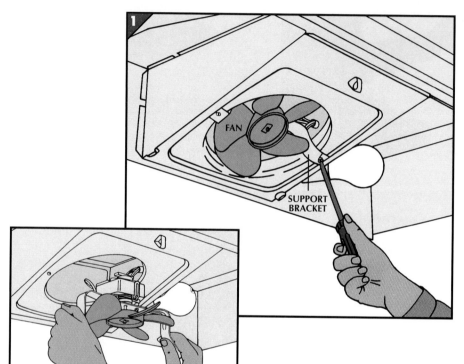

1. Removing the fan.
◆ First, turn off power to the range hood. Then remove the aluminum grease filter, which is secured by clips.
◆ To release the fan, remove the screws that hold the support bracket to the housing *(left)*.
◆ Holding the fan assembly by its support bracket, lower it from the housing *(inset)*.

2. Oiling and cleaning the fan.
◆ Hold the fan by its support bracket, and put a few drops of oil on the motor shaft at the rear of the fan *(right)*. Even permanently lubricated motors benefit from a few drops of machine oil.
◆ Wipe the fan motor and blades with a cloth moistened with a kitchen cleaner that contains ammonia.
◆ Before reinstalling the fan, clean the range hood surfaces and as much of the ductwork as you can reach.
◆ To reassemble the range hood, screw the support bracket to the fan housing, and reattach the grease filter.

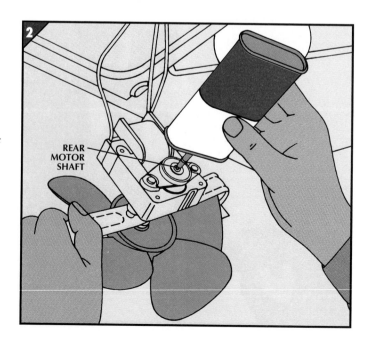

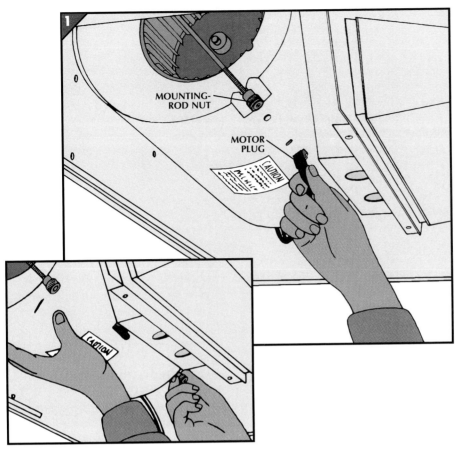

MOUNTING-
ROD NUT

MOTOR
PLUG

CAUTION

CAUTION

1. Removing the filters and blower assembly.
◆ With power to the range hood turned off, pull out the aluminum grease filters at both ends of the blower cover, and wash them in hot, soapy water.
◆ Remove the screws holding the cover in place, and take it off to expose the blower assembly.
◆ Unplug the motor as shown at left.
◆ Supporting the blower assembly with one hand, loosen the mounting-rod nuts on both sides *(inset)*.
◆ Move the rods out of the brackets, and lower the blower assembly.

2. Cleaning the impellers.
◆ With a hex wrench, loosen the setscrews holding the squirrel-cage blower impellers to the motor shaft.
◆ Grip the hub of each impeller in turn and slide it off the shaft. Use locking pliers, if necessary, to free balky impellers.
◆ Wash the squirrel cages in hot, soapy water, then replace them on the motor shaft and tighten the setscrews.
◆ Clean the interior of the range hood and as much of the ductwork as you can reach.
◆ To reinstall the blower assembly, lift it into position under the hood, keeping the discharge vent aligned with the duct opening.
◆ Slip the mounting rods into the brackets and tighten the nuts by hand.
◆ Plug in the motor, then screw the cover in place and reinsert the two grease filters.

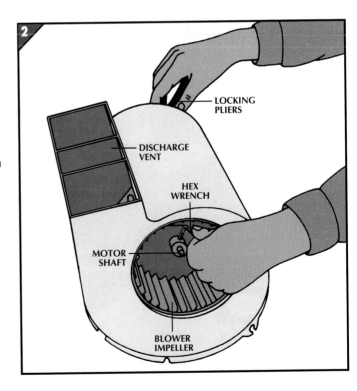

LOCKING
PLIERS

DISCHARGE
VENT

HEX
WRENCH

MOTOR
SHAFT

BLOWER
IMPELLER

Refrigerators usually provide years of trouble-free service. When a problem does arise, you can often make the diagnosis and repairs without any special tools.

Common Problems: A refrigerator usually signals a malfunction by not cooling or by making too much noise. There are many possible causes for a cooling failure, some of them quite simple (*see Troubleshooting Guide, right*). Before taking things apart, make sure that the door closes all the way and that the interior light (which produces heat) switches off properly. You should

see the light go off just as the door of the refrigerator closes.

A refrigerator that makes a screeching or rattling sound probably has a faulty evaporator or condenser fan motor. Replace a motor rather than trying to lubricate or repair it. Repairs to the compressor, evaporator, or condenser, which require special skills and tools, should be left to professionals.

Side-by-Sides and Icemakers: The parts of a side-by-side refrigerator may be located in places other than those shown on these pages, but the methods for testing and re-

pairing them remain the same.

Many refrigerators include an icemaker or fittings for installing one. Problems that commonly occur with these devices are leaks and loose shutoff arms; for repair instructions, see page 60.

⚠️ **CAUTION** *Before starting any repair, always unplug the refrigerator or shut off the power at the house service panel. After the repair, wait 15 minutes before plugging in the refrigerator. This delay allows pressures in the cooling system to equalize, lessening the start-up strain on the compressor.*

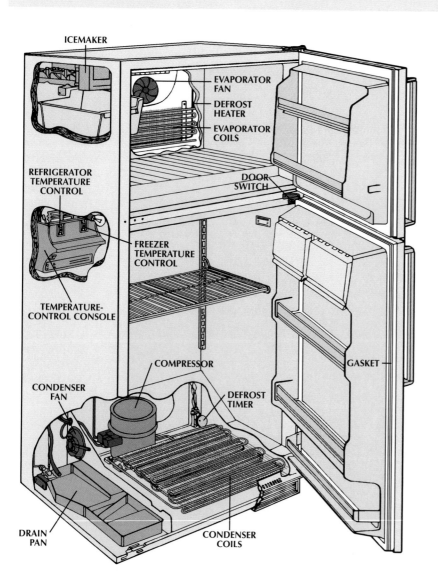

ICEMAKER

EVAPORATOR FAN

DEFROST HEATER

EVAPORATOR COILS

DOOR SWITCH

REFRIGERATOR TEMPERATURE CONTROL

FREEZER TEMPERATURE CONTROL

TEMPERATURE-CONTROL CONSOLE

COMPRESSOR

GASKET

CONDENSER FAN

DEFROST TIMER

DRAIN PAN

CONDENSER COILS

Anatomy of a refrigerator-freezer.

The cooling process begins when liquid refrigerant passes through the evaporator coils in the freezer, where it absorbs heat and becomes a gas. The refrigerant then flows to the compressor, which pumps it into the condenser coils. Cooled by air from the condenser fan, it releases its heat, returns to a liquid state, and begins the cycle again.

An evaporator fan circulates cold air within the freezer and, through vents, to the refrigerator area. A temperature control in the freezer regulates the airflow. Another in the refrigerator sets a thermostat that switches the compressor on and off to maintain the proper temperature in both compartments. Gaskets on the doors seal cold air inside. A door switch controls the light in the refrigerator compartment that comes on when the door is opened.

To prevent ice buildup, a defrost heater activated by a timer melts frost from the evaporator coils. A defrost-limit switch turns off the heater before the freezer gets too warm. Meltwater flows down a tube in the back wall and into a drain pan underneath.

Troubleshooting Guide

PROBLEM	REMEDY
Refrigerator not cold enough.	Test thermostat *(page 57)*. Clean condenser coils *(page 54)*. Replace the gasket *(page 55)* if door seal is not tight. Remove and test the door switch *(page 56)*. Replace evaporator fan *(page 57)*. Test defroster components; replace faulty ones *(page 59)*.
Refrigerator too cold.	Test thermostat *(page 57)*
Refrigerator doesn't run, but light works.	Test thermostat *(page 57)*. Clean condenser coils *(page 54)*. Check condenser fan and motor *(page 58)*. Test defrost timer *(page 59)*.
Refrigerator starts and stops frequently.	Clean condenser coils *(page 54)*. Check condenser fan and motor *(page 58)*.
Refrigerator runs constantly. See "Freezer doesn't defrost automatically" (below).	Replace the gasket *(page 55)* if door seal is not tight. Clean condenser coils *(page 54)*. Remove and test the door switch *(page 56)*. Check condenser fan and motor *(page 58)*.
Moisture around refrigerator door or frame.	Reset energy-saver switch. Replace the gasket *(page 55)* if door seal is not tight.
Ice in drain pan or water in bottom of refrigerator.	Clean drain hole *(page 54)*.
Water on floor around refrigerator.	Reposition drain pan. Clean drain hole *(page 54)*.
Interior light doesn't work.	Replace bulb, or test the door switch *(page 56)*.
Refrigerator noisy.	Reposition drain pan. Check condenser fan and motor *(page 58)*. Replace evaporator fan *(page 57)*.
Freezer doesn't defrost automatically.	Test defroster components; replace faulty ones *(page 59)*.
Icemaker doesn't make ice.	Open cold-water-supply valve fully or check water inlet valve *(page 60)*. Set freezer to colder temperature. Test icemaker's thermostat *(page 61)*. Test water inlet valve solenoid *(page 60)*.
Icemaker doesn't stop making ice.	Reseat a loose shutoff arm; test on/off switch *(page 61)*.
Water on the floor behind the refrigerator.	Tighten water inlet valve connections behind refrigerator.
Water overflows from icemaker.	Test water inlet valve and switch *(page 60)*; replace if necessary.
Icemaker doesn't eject ice cubes.	Test holding switch *(page 61)* and icemaker's thermostat *(page 61)*.

Dusting cooling-system components.

Condenser coils and metal cooling fins, which are best cleaned twice a year, are located either at the bottom front *(left)* or on the back of the appliance. To dust bottom-mounted coils, remove the floor-level grille. Use a long-handled brush to dust the coils and fins, taking care not to bend them. Vacuum up debris.

To expose the coils and fins on the back of a refrigerator, roll or walk the appliance away from the wall. Brush dust from the coils and fins, or use a vacuum cleaner with an upholstery-brush attachment.

BASIC REPAIRS FOR DOORS AND DRAINS

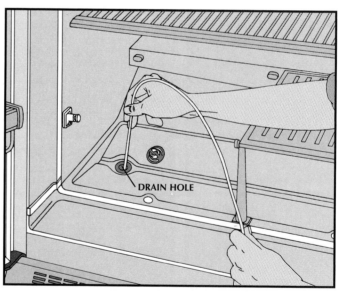

Adjusting a sagging freezer door.

◆ Using a nut driver or a socket wrench, loosen the two hex-headed bolts in the hinge at the top of the freezer door *(above)*.

◆ Reposition the door squarely over the opening of the freezer compartment by pulling upward on the door handle. Hold the door firmly in place and tighten the hinge bolts.

◆ Check the new position by opening and closing the door several times. It should clear the refrigerator door and align with the top of the unit.

Unclogging the drain hole.

◆ Remove the storage bins at the bottom of the refrigerator compartment to expose the drain hole, if there is one. Pry out the stopper plug with a screwdriver.

◆ Clear the drain by inserting a length of flexible $\frac{1}{4}$-inch plastic tubing or a pipe cleaner into the hole and pushing it through the drain canal into the drain pan *(above)*.

◆ Flush the drain with a solution of soapy water and ammonia, forcing it through the canal with a baster.

◆ Empty and wash the drain pan.

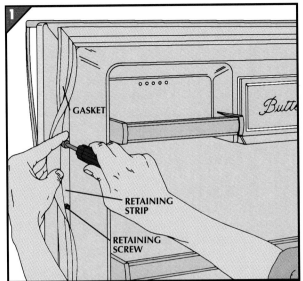

1. Loosening the retaining screws.

◆ Starting at the top outer corner of the door, roll back the rubber gasket with one hand, exposing the metal retaining strip beneath *(left)*.

◆ Use a nut driver to loosen the retaining screws two turns. Working across the top of the door and one-third of the way down each side of it, loosen each of the screws an equal amount.

GASKET

RETAINING STRIP

RETAINING SCREW

TRICKS OF THE TRADE

Getting the Wrinkles Out

New gaskets come folded in boxes and are usually kinked and wrinkled. Before installing one, you must straighten it. There are two effective ways to do so: Spread the gasket out in the sun on the hood of a car on a warm day, or soak it a little at a time in a skillet or pan of boiling water *(left)*. Allow a few hours for the first approach. Boiling water should unkink the gasket immediately.

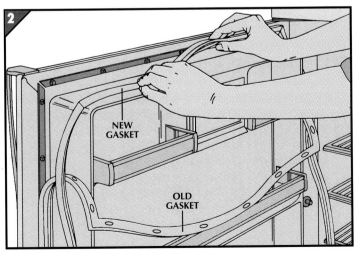

2. Installing a new gasket.

◆ Pull the old gasket straight up to free it from behind the retaining strip at the top of the door.

◆ Let the old gasket hang out of the way, and slide the new gasket behind the retaining strip *(left)*, beginning along the top of the door and working down the sides. Partially tighten the screws.

◆ Working down each side, loosen the screws and strip off the old gasket; then insert the new gasket and partially tighten the screws.

◆ At the bottom of the door, slip out the old gasket at one corner, and replace it with the new gasket before loosening the retaining screws at the other corner. Then complete the last few inches of the installation.

NEW GASKET

OLD GASKET

3. Squaring the door.

◆ Close the door and look for gaps between the gasket and the body of the refrigerator. Usually found on the handle side of the door, a gap indicates a slight twist in the door, introduced during gasket installation.

◆ If the door is twisted, open it and have a partner push on the top or bottom of the doorframe to counter the twist. If you don't have any help, support the door with your foot *(left)* while pushing on the frame. Tighten the screws once the door looks straight.

◆ If a gap still shows when you close the door, open it again, loosen the screws a half-turn, and repeat the squaring process.

A NEW DOOR SWITCH

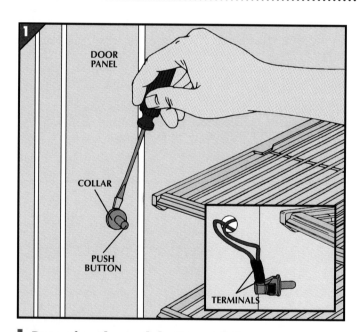

DOOR PANEL

COLLAR

PUSH BUTTON

TERMINALS

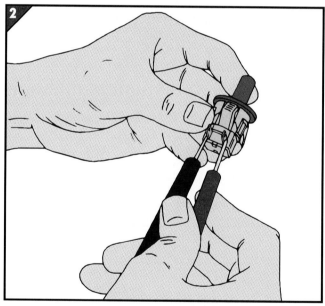

1. Removing the push-button switch.

◆ Unplug the refrigerator, cover a screwdriver tip with masking tape, then gently pry the collar encircling the push button from the door panel.

◆ Tilt the push button so you can get the right-angle terminals through the hole *(inset)*, then pull the switch out of the door panel along with its wires.

2. Checking switch operation.

◆ Pull the wires off the terminals and, using a multi-tester, test the switch for resistance *(page 31)*. The switch should show 0 ohms when the push button is up *(above)* and infinite ohms when it is depressed.

◆ Replace a faulty switch by attaching the wires to the new switch and inserting it into the hole in the door panel.

REGAINING CONTROL OF THE TEMPERATURE

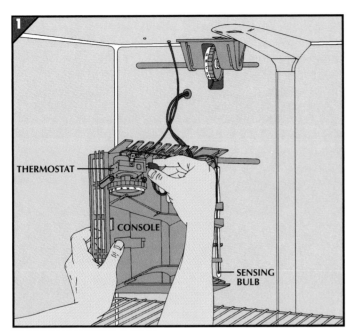

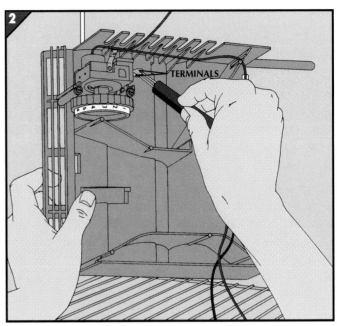

1. Getting at the thermostat.
◆ Unplug the refrigerator and unscrew the temperature-control console. For a control recessed into the top of the compartment, unscrew the breaker strips securing the console and remove it.
◆ Disconnect the wires that are attached to the thermostat terminals (above).
◆ Rest the console on a shelf, taking care not to bend the tube of the sensing bulb.

2. Putting the thermostat through its paces.
◆ Test the thermostat for resistance (page 31) by turning the control dial to OFF and touching a multitester's probes to the two terminals (above); the meter should show infinite resistance.
◆ With the probes still touching the terminals, turn the dial to ON and gradually rotate it toward the coldest setting. The meter should show 0 ohms at some point. If it does not, replace the thermostat.

A MOTOR FOR THE EVAPORATOR FAN

1. Gaining access to the fan.
◆ Unplug the refrigerator and remove the icemaker and any shelves from the freezer.
◆ On some models, you must unscrew and remove a fan grille to get at the rear panel. If the grille is also secured by plastic tabs at the freezer floor, bend the grille gently inward to free it from one tab at a time.
◆ Unscrew the freezer's rear panel to reveal the evaporator coils and fan. Lift out the panel (left) with its insulation, if any. Cover the exposed evaporator fins with a towel before beginning work on the fan.

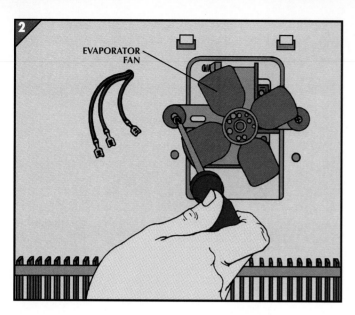

2. A new fan.

◆ If the fan's plastic grille is located behind the rear panel, unscrew it and remove it.

◆ Disconnect the wires from the fan motor, remove the screws that secure the fan to the cabinet *(left)*, and pull out the fan assembly.

◆ Before discarding the old fan, unscrew the blades from the motor shaft. Examine them for cracks and replace them if they are damaged; otherwise reuse them.

◆ Secure the fan blades on the shaft of the new motor, then insert the fan in the opening located at the back of the freezer, positioned so that the terminals face the loose wires.

◆ Screw the fan to the cabinet, reattach the wires, and replace the fan grille. Reinstall the rear panel, as well as any equipment removed earlier.

RENEWED AIRFLOW TO THE CONDENSER

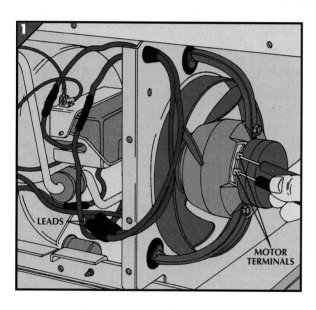

1. Testing the motor.

◆ Unplug the refrigerator, move it away from the wall, and remove the rear access panel.

◆ Spin the condenser fan to see if it turns freely. If it does not, the motor bearings are worn; replace the motor *(Step 2)*.

◆ If the fan turns without binding, disconnect the wire leads from the motor and test it for resistance at the terminals *(left)*. With a multitester set at RX1, the meter should read between 200 and 500 ohms; a reading other than that means that the motor should be replaced.

2. Replacing a faulty motor.

◆ With the refrigerator unplugged, unscrew the condenser fan's mounting brackets from the divider panel *(right)* and lift out the fan assembly.

◆ Unfasten the mounting bracket from the motor and remove the hub nut that holds the fan blades in place.

◆ Wash the blades if they are dirty.

◆ Attach both the blades and the bracket to a new motor, then align the fan assembly in the refrigerator and screw the bracket to the divider panel.

◆ Reconnect the leads to the terminals.

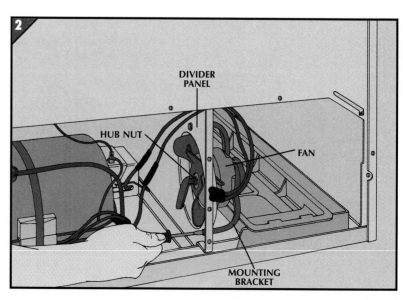

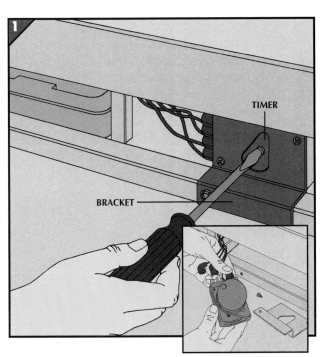

1. Trying the defrost timer.

◆ Locate the defrost timer, which may be behind the bottom front grille or rear access panel, or in the temperature-control console.
◆ With the compressor running, insert a screwdriver blade in the timer slot *(left)* and turn it clockwise until it clicks. If the compressor stops and the freezer begins defrosting, you have a faulty timer.
◆ To replace a timer, unplug the refrigerator and unscrew the timer's mounting bracket. Unscrew the timer from the bracket. If a ground wire is attached to the cabinet, disconnect it. Pull the wires from the timer terminals one by one *(inset),* transferring each to the corresponding terminal on the new timer.
◆ Screw the new timer to the mounting bracket and reconnect the ground wire. Reinstall the timer on the refrigerator frame.

2. Checking the defrost heater.

◆ With the power off, remove the rear panel to reveal the defrost heater—a glass or steel tube that runs behind the evaporator coils and often along the sides. (If the heater is embedded in the coils, leave servicing to a trained technician.) Tighten loose wires to the heater and replace burned ones.

◆ Test resistance *(page 32)* by removing the wires and touching multitester probes to the terminals *(left).* A reading between 5 and 100 ohms indicates a functional heater.
◆ To replace a defective heater, put on gloves for protection against sharp evaporator fins. Twist the tabs holding the heater in its brackets, remove it, and clip in the new one.

3. Replacing the defrost-limit switch.

◆ If the other defrost components are working, replace the defrost-limit switch; it is usually above or attached to the coils.
◆ Unscrew or unclip the switch and pull off the wire connectors if they are detachable; otherwise cut the wires to the switch and connect a new switch with wire caps *(right).*
◆ Squeeze silicone caulking into the wire caps' base to protect the connections from moisture.
◆ Clip or screw the switch in place, then replace the insulation and the rear panel.

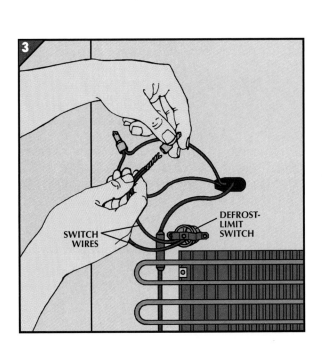

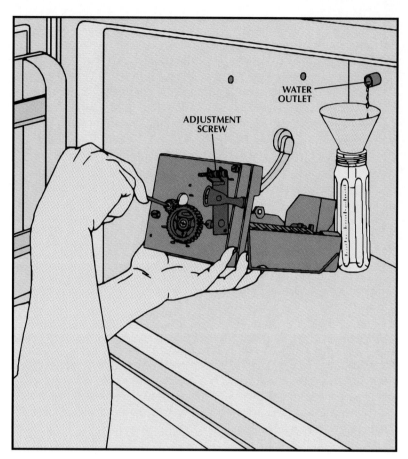

Adjusting the water fill.

◆ Remove the icemaker cover, and if your ice-maker has no label warning against rotating the drive gear on the front of the device, unscrew the unit from the freezer. Do not unplug it. If there is a warning label, try turning the water-adjustment screw as needed.

◆ Put a small funnel in the mouth of a baby bottle or other container marked in ounces and place it under the water outlet.

◆ Insert a screwdriver in the gear slot *(left)* and gently turn the gear counterclockwise about a half-turn, until you hear the motor start.

◆ Allow the unit to complete a cycle, then check the level of the water in the bottle; it should be about 5 ounces.

◆ Increase or reduce the water flow by turning the water-adjustment screw a small amount toward the + or - sign. Run another test cycle to check your adjustment.

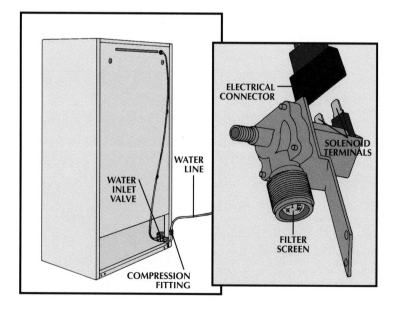

Correcting the water flow.

◆ Close the valve in the water line to the refrigerator and remove the rear access panel to expose the water inlet valve. Place a shallow pan under the line to catch drips, and unscrew the compression fitting at the valve. Discard the used brass ring from the fitting, and obtain a new one for the reinstallation.

◆ Unplug the refrigerator, pull the electrical connector from the water inlet valve *(inset)*, and test the resistance between the solenoid terminals *(page 32)*. If the reading is less than 60 ohms or more than 500 ohms, replace the valve.

◆ If the resistance falls within these limits, try cleaning the filter screen. Remove any screws on the valve and take it apart; scrape the screen, rinse it well, and reassemble the valve.

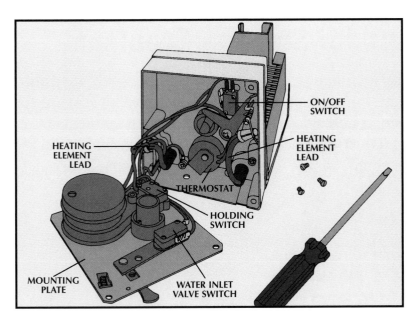

ON/OFF SWITCH

HEATING ELEMENT LEAD

HEATING ELEMENT LEAD

THERMOSTAT

HOLDING SWITCH

MOUNTING PLATE

WATER INLET VALVE SWITCH

Testing the electrical components.

◆ Unplug the icemaker and remove its cover and mounting plate. To check the thermostat for resistance *(page 31)*, leave the icemaker in the freezer. Remove the heating element leads and touch a probe to each terminal; at temperatures below 15° F., you should get 0 ohms. Retest the icemaker at room temperature. It should read more than 0; if not, replace the thermostat.

◆ Unscrew a clamp to remove the thermostat. Put metallic putty on the back of the new thermostat and stick it down. Screw in the clamp.

◆ To test a switch, disconnect its leads and unscrew the switch. Test each terminal against its common contact (marked "C"); when the switch button is down, one terminal should show 0 ohms, the other more than 0. Readings should be opposite when the button is up.

REPLACING AN ICEMAKER SHUTOFF ARM

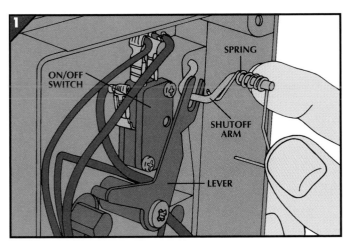

SPRING

ON/OFF SWITCH

SHUTOFF ARM

LEVER

1. Reseating the spring and arm.

◆ Unplug the refrigerator, take out the icemaker, and remove the mounting plate.

◆ Check that the spring is engaged on the shutoff arm *(left)* and that the arm is in the slot in the end of the lever that links it to the on/off switch. If necessary, seat the spring as shown and put the arm back in the slot.

◆ If the shutoff mechanism still does not work, replace the shutoff arm *(below)*.

2. Replacing the shutoff arm.

◆ Carefully disengage the spring and separate the old arm from the lever. Push the arm forward, turning it as required to work it out through the hole in the housing *(right)*.

◆ Slide the new shutoff arm through the front of the housing. Engage the arm in the lever slot and replace the spring *(above)*.

◆ Replace the mounting plate and cover, and reinstall the icemaker.

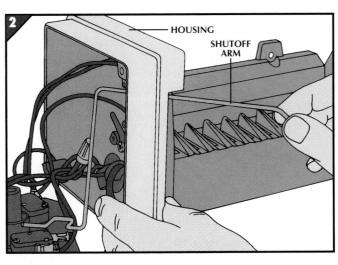

HOUSING

SHUTOFF ARM

Custom Solutions for Storage Problems

3

No matter how large your kitchen, it never seems to have enough space for everything you need to store. Often, the solution is to organize the available space for greater efficiency. Options range from adding simple screw-on attachments to restructuring cabinet interiors. Or, from a pair of cabinets, you can build a handy movable island that increases both storage capacity and counter space.

Stow-Away Recycling Bins →

Whether your kitchen cabinets are old or new, you can make them more efficient and increase their capacity with attachments and ready-made space organizers.

External Attachments: If you know the manufacturer of your cabinets, the local dealer can supply a catalog showing current kits and accessories. The kits come with hardware, instructions, and templates to make installation easy.

The underside of a wall cabinet lends itself to space-saving accessories such as a swing-out cookbook holder or a hanging glass rack that keeps fine stemware protected yet easy to reach.

Internal Modifications: You can also transform drawers and storage spaces in base cabinets. A tilt-out tray at the sink front keeps items like sponges, brushes, and rubber gloves right where you need them. A conventional drawer box with a removable front can be replaced

with a combination cutlery tray and pull-out cutting board.

The ample storage space in blind corner cabinets is often wasted because it is so hard to reach. Half-moon shelves that pivot as a lazy Susan does and then slide out on glides give easy access to the deepest recesses of the cabinet.

Most modern cabinets have removable shelves, which simplifies converting the interior space to another purpose. Permanent shelves need to be cut out *(page 68)*. With the cabinet space cleared, you can choose whichever of the units profiled on the following pages suit your particular needs.

Ensuring Correct Fit: Knowing the exact dimensions of drawers and cabinet openings will help you pick accessories that fit perfectly. To make sure racks, shelves, and glide-out trays will be absolutely level, always check screw hole locations with a carpenter's level before you drill pilot holes.

TOOLS

Screwdriver	Awl
Power drill	Saber saw
Tape measure	Combination square
Carpenter's level	

SIMPLE ATTACHMENTS TO A CABINET FRAME

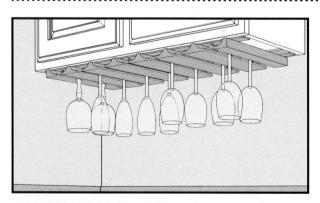 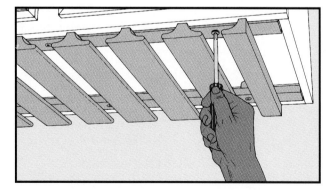

A hanging stemware rack.
◆ Hold the preassembled wooden rack in place under the cabinet and mark with a pencil through the predrilled screw holes in the mounting rail. Drill a pilot hole at each mark with a $\frac{3}{32}$-inch twist bit, making

sure not to drill through the cabinet bottom.
◆ Insert a $1\frac{1}{2}$-inch No. 8 wood screw through each hole in the rail, and slip plastic spacers over each screw. Then drive the screws into the pilot holes *(above)*.

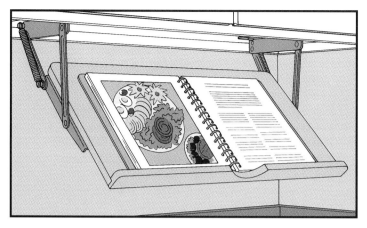

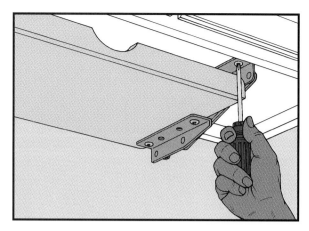

A retractable cookbook rack.

◆ Place the rack against the cabinet bottom with the spring-loaded hinges in a closed position and the front edge of the hinge plates $\frac{1}{2}$ inch behind the overhanging lip of the cabinet face. Outline the location of the hinge plates on the cabinet bottom with a pencil.

◆ Open the rack and reposition the hinge at the penciled outline. Mark the location of the hinge screws and drill $\frac{3}{32}$-inch pilot holes. Fasten the holder to the cabinet with the screws provided (above, right).

A TILT-OUT TRAY IN THE SINK APRON

1. Attaching hinges to the cabinet frame.

◆ Reach up through the cabinet door below the sink to find the opening in the cabinet face directly in front of the sink. With a pencil, trace the opening on the back of the decorative face panel, then unscrew the panel from the cabinet.

◆ Position the left-hand hinge flush with the cabinet face and $\frac{3}{32}$ inch above the bottom of the opening. Mark the location for the hinge screws at the center of the oblong holes in the hinge plate and drill $\frac{3}{32}$-inch pilot holes at the marks.

◆ Fasten the hinge to the frame without tightening the screws all the way (left). Repeat for the right-hand hinge.

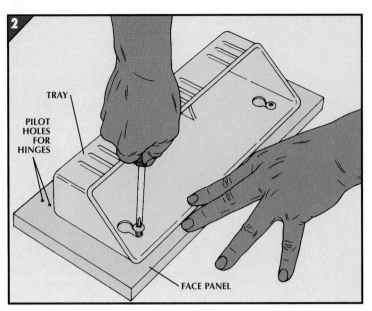

2. Attaching the tray.

◆ With the hinges extended from the cabinet, align the hinge plates with the bottom of the penciled outline on the face panel. Mark the screw holes and drill pilot holes. If a handle is provided, center it on the front of the panel, then mark and drill those holes, too.

◆ Lay the front panel facedown on a worktable and center the tray $\frac{1}{8}$ inch below the penciled line that indicates the top of the cabinet opening. On the panel, make a mark at the narrow end of each of the tray's two keyhole-shaped slots.

◆ Drill pilot holes at the marks, then screw two $\frac{1}{2}$-inch panhead screws into the holes just deep enough to allow the tray to slide over them *(left)*. Set the tray aside for now.

3. Remounting the face panel.

◆ Attach the handle, if there is one, to the front of the panel.

◆ Screw the panel to the hinges without tightening the screws completely. If the countertop is in the way, use a stubby screwdriver as shown at right.

◆ Adjust the position of the hinges so the panel fits flush against the cabinet face and is parallel to the countertop, then tighten all the hinge screws. Finally, slip the tray onto the mounting screws on the inside of the panel.

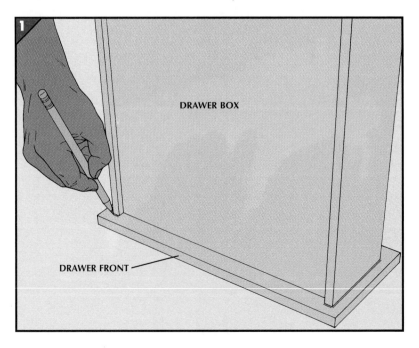

A COMBINATION CUTLERY DRAWER AND CUTTING BOARD

1. Marking the drawer face.

◆ Remove the drawer by pulling it open and lifting it slightly to disengage the metal glides from their channels inside the cabinet.

◆ Trace the outline of the sides and bottom of the drawer box on the back of the drawer front *(right)*. Remove the screws that hold the box to the front, but do not remove the drawer handle if there is one.

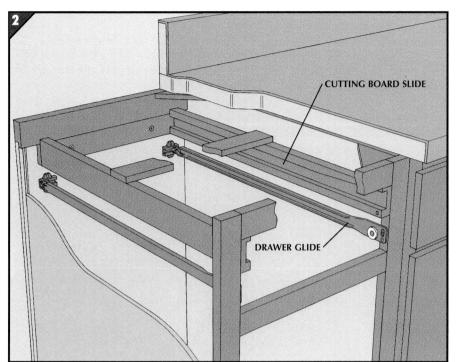

2. Installing the cutting board.

◆ Insert the cutting board slide into the drawer opening. Hold its upper surface against the opening's top and its front flush with the cabinet face.

◆ Mark the inside of the cabinet for pilot holes by pushing an awl through the predrilled screw holes on the sides and the back rail of the assembly. Remove the assembly and drill $\frac{3}{32}$-inch pilot holes.

◆ Screw the cutting board slide to the cabinet, then insert the cutting board.

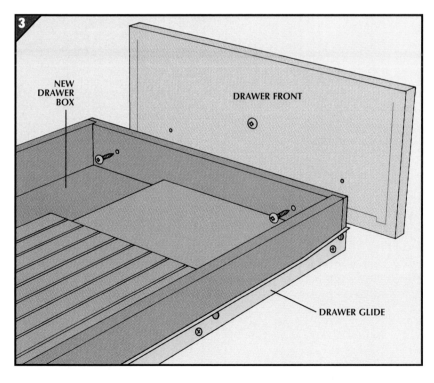

3. Attaching the cutlery tray.

◆ Set the front of the new drawer box with the cutlery tray against the back of the drawer front, aligning the bottom and sides of the box on the corresponding outline of the old drawer. Mark the drawer front through the predrilled screw holes at the front of the tray. Drill pilot holes and attach the box to the drawer front.

◆ The drawer box comes with metal glides that match those of the original drawer box. Tilt the box into the cabinet opening and slip the rollers at the rear of the glides into the channels in the cabinet.

REMOVING CABINET SHELVES

1. Cutting a fixed shelf.

◆ Using a saber saw fitted with a flush-cutting blade, cut a wedge from the shelf as shown at left. Tape a scrap of metal to the back of the cabinet to protect it from the saw blade.

◆ Tap the top and bottom of the shelf around the edges with a hammer several times to break the glue bond that holds the shelf in the dado joint.

2. Taking out the pieces.

◆ Gently work each half of the shelf up and down until it comes loose, then remove it. If necessary, cut each piece in half, parallel to the cabinet front, to facilitate removal.

◆ Fill the dado joint with wood putty and let dry. Then sand it with fine-grit sandpaper until it is flush with the cabinet wall.

VERTICAL DIVIDERS FOR HARD-TO-STORE ITEMS

Installing vertical dividers.

◆ Cut lengths of metal, plastic, or wood tracks as long as the cabinet is deep. Screw tracks to the cabinet bottom, perpendicular to the cabinet face, at about 4-inch intervals. Also cut $\frac{3}{8}$-inch plywood panels equal in width to the cabinet depth and $\frac{1}{4}$ inch shorter than the door opening.

◆ If the cabinet door opening has no frame *(far left)*, slide a panel fitted with a top track into each bottom track. Holding the panel vertical, draw position lines for the upper track, then screw it to the cabinet top.

◆ For a framed door opening *(left)*, hang the top tracks between the bottom edge of the frame and a crosswise board screwed to the rear wall.

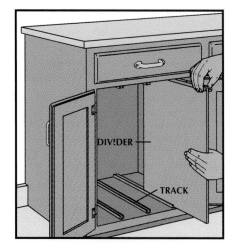

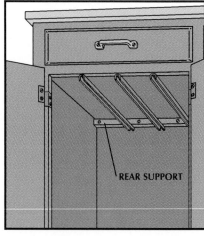

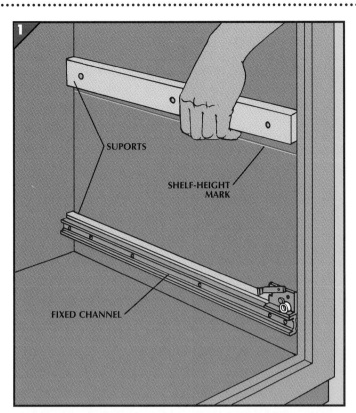

SUPORTS

SHELF-HEIGHT MARK

FIXED CHANNEL

1. Mounting the glides.
◆ Mark both cabinet side walls at the height you have chosen for shelves.
◆ Cut glide supports to match the depth of the cabinet. Use stock no thinner than the distance from the door opening to the adjacent cabinet wall. Plane the pieces to this thickness as needed.
◆ Bore screw holes 6 inches apart in each support. Align the bottom edge of a support with a shelf-height mark and drill pilot holes into the cabinet. Glue and screw the supports in place.
◆ Mount the fixed channels of the drawer glides flush with the bottom of the supports.

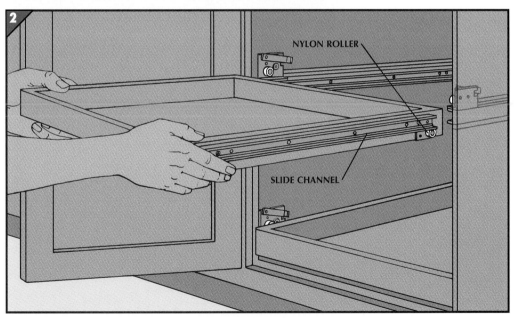

NYLON ROLLER

SLIDE CHANNEL

2. Installing the shelf.
◆ Align the slide channel of the drawer glide so that the nylon roller is flush with the bottom edge of the drawer *(above)*. Drill pilot holes, then screw the slide channel to the drawer.
◆ Repeat for the other side of the drawer, then position the nylon rollers in the fixed channel and push the drawer into the cabinet.

A HIDDEN RECYCLING BIN

1. Marking the door position.
◆ First, lightly outline the door on the cabinet face with a pencil *(left),* then unscrew the door from the hinges and set it aside.
◆ Remove the hinges from the cabinet frame and fill the holes with wood filler of a color similar to the cabinet finish. To avoid damaging the finish, do not sand the filler.

2. Centering the wire frame in the cabinet.
◆ Attach the wire frame of the recycling bin to the slide channels of the glides with a hex wrench *(right).*
◆ Place the assembly in the cabinet, centering it in the opening and making certain that the front edge of the wire frame is parallel to the face of the cabinet.
◆ With a pencil, mark the screw holes for the glides on the cabinet floor.

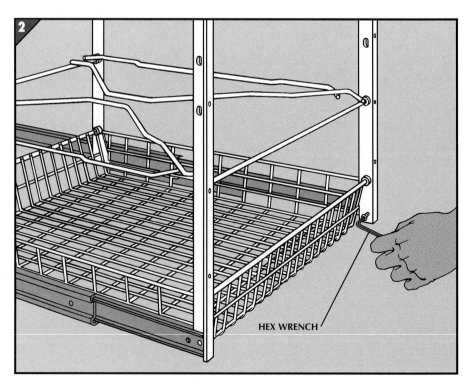

HEX WRENCH

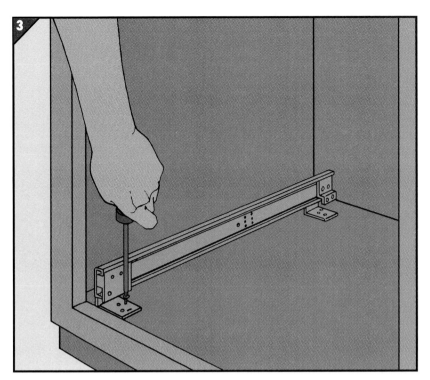

3. Attaching the glides.

◆ Remove the assembly and unscrew the wire frame from the glides.

◆ Drill pilot holes at the pencil marks and screw the glides to the cabinet floor *(left)*.

◆ Extend the inner channels of the glides from the cabinet, then set the wire frame between them.

◆ Starting at the back, reattach the frame to the glides.

4. Measuring the door position.

◆ Push the wire frame in until it is flush with the cabinet face. Hold a combination square against the cabinet and measure the distance between the penciled door outline and the center of a mounting hole in the recycling bin frame *(right)*. Then slide the square body to that point on the ruler.

◆ Using the square to guide a pencil down the inside of the door *(inset)*, draw a line along both vertical edges.

◆ On the cabinet, measure down from the top pencil outline to the first hole on the wire frame, and mark this distance on both of the lines drawn with the square on the door. Drill a pilot hole at each mark.

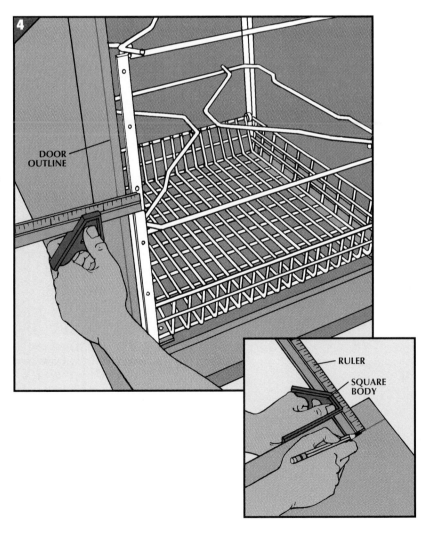

DOOR OUTLINE

RULER

SQUARE BODY

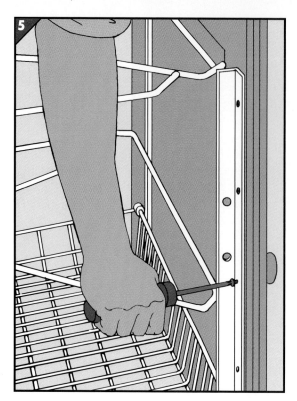

5. Attaching the door.

◆ Pull out the wire frame and have a helper hold the door against it. Drive a screw in each of the two pilot holes, then close the door and make sure it is square on the cabinet face.

◆ Open the door and mark it for the remaining screws, using holes in the wire frame as a guide. Drill pilot holes and drive the screws.

◆ Finally, place the plastic recycling bins in the wire frame.

HALF-MOON SHELVES FOR A CORNER

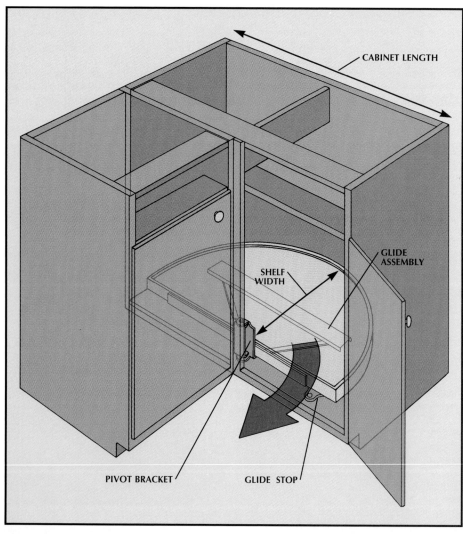

CABINET LENGTH

SHELF WIDTH

GLIDE ASSEMBLY

PIVOT BRACKET   GLIDE STOP

Getting the right size.

The glide assembly that supports a half-moon shelf pivots on a bracket attached to the cabinet frame. A glide stop prevents the shelf from being pushed into the cabinet too far and bumping the wall. A wheel on the glide stop blocks the hardware from marring the cabinet door when the shelf is pulled out.

Three cabinet dimensions govern shelf size: depth, length, and the width of the door opening. The standard cabinet depth is 24 inches, but door openings and lengths vary. A good rule of thumb is to buy a shelf 3 inches shorter than the length of the cabinet and about 1 inch narrower than the width of the door opening.

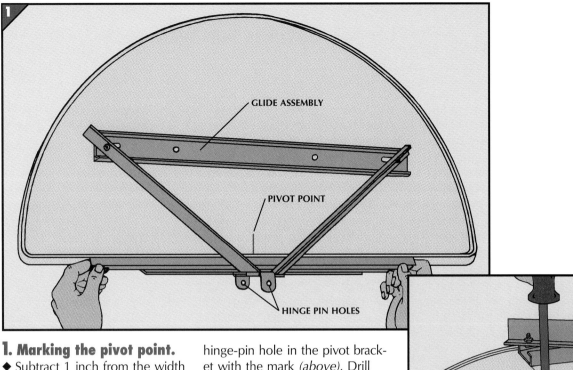

GLIDE ASSEMBLY

PIVOT POINT

HINGE PIN HOLES

GLIDE STOP

1. Marking the pivot point.
◆ Subtract 1 inch from the width of the cabinet door opening. Mark this distance on the bottom of the shelf, measuring from the end that will be farthest from the door opening after the unit is installed.
◆ Hold the glide assembly against the shelf and align the hinge-pin hole in the pivot bracket with the mark *(above)*. Drill pilot holes into the bottom and the edge of the shelf and attach the glide.
◆ Next, mount the glide stop on the bottom of the shelf at the end of the glide nearest the cabinet opening *(inset)*.

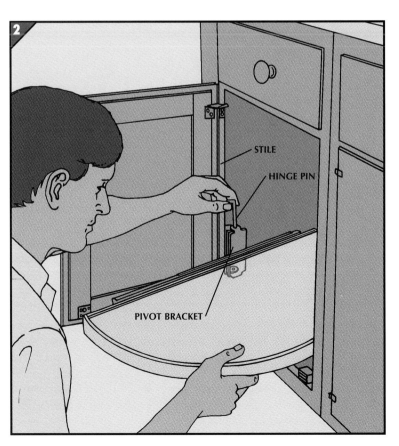

STILE

HINGE PIN

PIVOT BRACKET

2. Installing the shelf.
◆ Hold the pivot bracket against the inside of the stile at the shelf height you have chosen, but no closer than $\frac{3}{4}$ inch from the cabinet bottom. Mark the screw positions, drill pilot holes, and mount the bracket on the cabinet.
◆ Hold the shelf in position to align the hinge-pin holes on both halves of the bracket, and drop the pin into place *(left)*.

No kitchen is complete without a selection of herbs and spices. Yet the small jars that hold these seasonings are a nuisance, wasting space on regular cabinet shelves or getting lost behind larger containers. The two simple projects shown here allow you to organize spice jars in their own separate space.

The door-mounted spice rack can be hung on any solid raised-panel or European-style cabinet door at least $\frac{3}{4}$ inch thick. Only 3 inches deep, the rack uses very little of the interior when the door is closed. Consider hanging two or three racks on the door, fitting them between the cabinet shelves.

A kitchen drawer that is at least $3\frac{1}{2}$ inches deep can accommodate an easy-to-build rack that provides convenient storage for standard 2-inch-diameter, $4\frac{1}{4}$-inch-tall spice jars. Any leftover space in the back of the drawer can house seldom-used utensils. Either of these spice racks can be painted or stained before it is installed.

TOOLS

Backsaw	Nail set
Miter box	Hammer
$\frac{1}{4}$-inch drill	Ruler

MATERIALS

1- by 3-inch clear pine

$\frac{1}{4}$- by $1\frac{3}{8}$-inch wood lath

$\frac{1}{4}$-inch hardwood dowel

$\frac{1}{4}$-inch plywood

$\frac{3}{4}$-inch quarter-round molding

Carpenter's glue

$\frac{5}{8}$-inch oval-head wood screws

$\frac{3}{4}$-inch brads

A DOOR-MOUNTED SPICE RACK

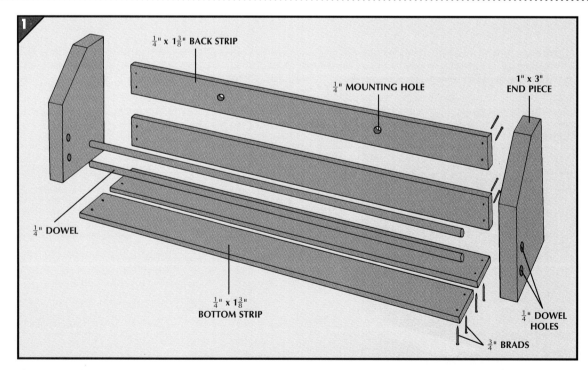

1. Measuring the pieces.
The diagram above shows the individual pieces that are required to assemble the spice rack. The two end pieces are made from one 10-inch length of pine, sawed in half. The back and bottom strips are thin pieces of wood called lath, and the front rails are made of hardwood dowel. The length of these pieces depends on the size of your cabinet.

◆ Measure the inside width of the cabinet door and subtract at least 2 inches to allow for clearance at each end of the rack. Note any hinges or hardware on the door or cabinet frame that might interfere, and adjust the width of the rack accordingly.

◆ Use this measurement to mark four lengths of the wood lath and two lengths of dowel.

BACK-SAW

MITER BOX

2. Cutting the wood lath and dowels.

◆ Place a backsaw in the miter box's right-angle slots. Hold the wood tightly against the side of the miter box with one hand, and saw through it with light, smooth strokes.

◆ Saw all four pieces of lath and the two dowels, then lay them side by side. Sand if necessary until all are the same length.

3. Making the end pieces.

◆ On a 10-inch length of 1-by-3 pine, measure and mark $1\frac{3}{4}$ inches from a corner in both directions. Using a straightedge, draw a line between the two marks *(below)*.

◆ Set the backsaw in the miter box's 45° slots, and saw along the line.

◆ Repeat this step at the other end, then cut the board squarely in half midway between the beveled ends.

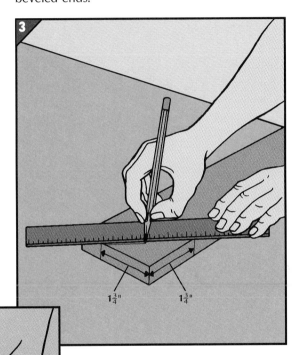

$1\frac{3}{4}$" $1\frac{3}{4}$"

BOTTOM EDGE

$\frac{3}{8}$"

1"

SCRAP WOOD

4. Drilling the dowel holes.

◆ On the face of each end piece, draw a straight line $\frac{3}{8}$ inch from, and parallel to, the shorter edge. Mark the line 1 and 2 inches from the bottom edge of the end piece.

◆ Hold the end piece down firmly on a piece of scrap wood, and drill a $\frac{1}{4}$-inch hole straight through the board's face at each mark.

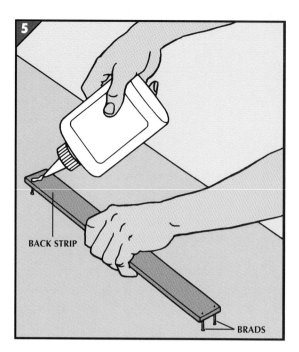

BACK STRIP

BRADS

5. Assembling the back.

◆ To attach the back strips, place a piece of lath on the scrap wood, and, $\frac{3}{8}$ inch from one end, tap down two $\frac{3}{4}$-inch brads until their tips emerge on the other side.

◆ Repeat at the other end, then squeeze a thin bead of glue across all the tips.

◆ Nail the lath to the back edge of each end piece, flush with the bottom.

◆ Prepare a second piece of lath the same way. Then measure $1\frac{3}{8}$ inches above the first strip, and nail the second strip to the back of the end piece.

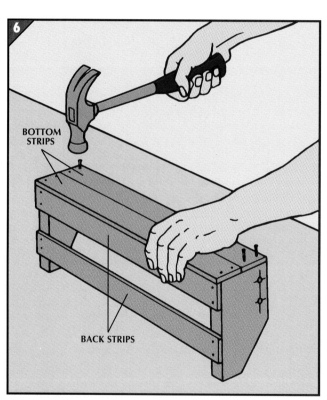

BOTTOM STRIPS

BACK STRIPS

6. Adding the bottom strips.

◆ Tap brads through the remaining two pieces of lath, and add glue as in Step 5.

◆ Then turn the rack upside down and nail one piece of lath to the bottom of the end piece, flush with the back strip.

◆ Nail the last piece to the bottom, flush with the front of the end piece *(above)*.

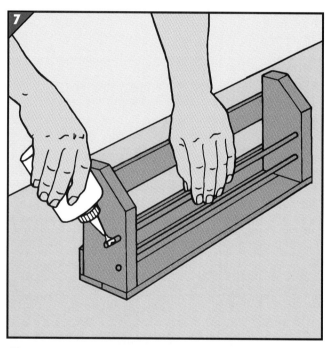

7. Gluing the dowels.

◆ Test-fit the dowels by sliding them through the holes in the end pieces; if a dowel binds, lightly sand it down.

◆ Pull the dowels out slightly and smear glue on their ends *(above)*, then push them in so that the ends are flush with the outer faces of the end pieces. Wipe off any excess glue and let dry.

◆ To mount the rack, drill two $\frac{1}{4}$-inch holes in the center of the upper back strip, 3 inches from each end.

◆ Hold the rack against the cabinet door, making sure it fits between the cabinet shelves, and mark the mounting holes on the door. Drill pilot holes at the marks, then attach the rack with $\frac{5}{8}$-inch oval-head wood screws.

CONVERTING A KITCHEN DRAWER TO A SPICE RACK

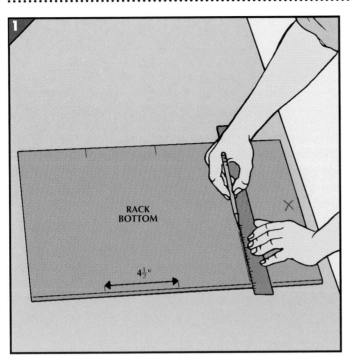

1. Laying out the rack.
◆ Measure the interior of the drawer bottom and subtract $\frac{1}{8}$ inch from the length and width. Then cut a piece of plywood—birch veneer plywood has a nice, smooth finish—to those dimensions for the rack bottom.
◆ Mark an X at what will be the bottom of the rack—that is, the edge nearest the drawer front. Starting at that edge, place marks along the sides of the plywood at $4\frac{1}{2}$-inch intervals.
◆ With a ruler or carpenter's square, draw parallel lines connecting the marks. You will need to make one divider for each line.

2. Cutting the dividers.
◆ Measure and mark pieces of $\frac{3}{4}$-inch quarter-round molding to match the width of the piece of plywood.
◆ Use a backsaw and the right-angle slots on a miter box to cut the pieces squarely.
◆ On each piece, tap $\frac{3}{4}$-inch brads into the center of the molding's round face at 5-inch intervals until the tips just protrude through the flat side.

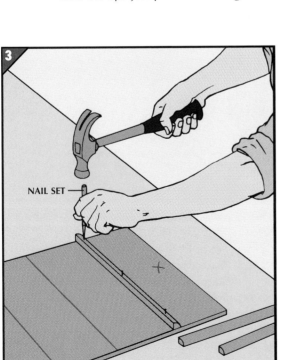

3. Final assembly.
◆ Take one of the dividers and squeeze a thin line of glue between the protruding tips.
◆ Place the divider on the first line above the X marking the rack bottom. The divider's 90° angle should be flush on the line, with the rounded face toward the bottom.
◆ Hammer the brads until their heads barely show, then use a nail set *(left)* to drive them just below the surface. Repeat this procedure with the remaining dividers.
◆ Fill the nail holes with wood putty, sand smooth, then finish as desired.

Making Deep Cabinets Accessible

The back part of a deep cabinet is often hard to reach and difficult to see, making it less than ideal for storage. To open up this space, you can build movable storage units that pivot on hinges or roll out on drawer glides. Tailored to fit your cabinet, these units can provide more accessible space for anything from canned goods to kitchen utensils.

A Swing-Out Shelf Unit: Pivoting on a hinge at one side to allow access to the back of the cabinet, this unit has shelves on front and back sized for standard jars and cans. The weight of its contents demands solid support, which you can provide by attaching its mounting cleat with screws long enough to penetrate into the side of an adjoining cabinet. To avoid excessive stress on the mounting hardware, do not load a swing-out unit with heavy items such as large juice cans.

Dual Bins: Side-by-side glide-out bins, with partitions and shelves that fit your needs, are more complicated to build but accommodate awkward items. In the examples on pages 82-87, one bin has a rear compartment for long-handled skillets and a front one for saucepans with space below for lids. The other bin combines shelves with a compartment for tall items and a top tray for large cutlery and other utensils.

Planning: The dimensions of the swing-out and glide-out units shown depend on the size of the original cabinets and your storage needs. The arrangement you choose may include shelves for cans and jars, trays for flatware, or compartments for tall items that are hard to store in conventional cabinets and drawers. In determining the number and spacing of shelves, allow at least 1 extra inch between shelves, to facilitate storing and removing objects.

If your existing cabinets have permanent shelves, you may need to cut them back *(page 80)* or remove them entirely *(page 68)* before installing a new storage unit.

Materials: Most of the parts of the units shown here are made of clear birch plywood, which has smooth surfaces that are easily prepared for painting or staining. The vertical pieces, which carry most of the structural loads, are made from $\frac{3}{4}$-inch plywood, as are the shelves for the swing-out unit. Shelves and rails for the dual bins are cut from $\frac{1}{2}$-inch sheets, and the broad panel that closes one side of a glide-out bin is made from lighter $\frac{1}{4}$-inch plywood. Cleats that support hinges or drawer glides are 1-by-2 clear pine.

Building Tips: When cutting plywood, use a circular saw with a plywood blade or a combination blade that makes both crosscuts and rip cuts. To insure the proper alignment of joints in the dual bins, cut the pieces with dadoes, rabbets, and cutouts first. Make the remaining pieces as you go along. For both units, hold pieces together with bar clamps while you drill pilot holes *(page 10)* for inconspicuous trimhead screws. Protect the unit's finish with scrap wood under the clamp. Test assemblies for fit and alignment before gluing.

 **TOOLS**

Bar clamps
Tape measure
$\frac{1}{4}$-inch or $\frac{3}{8}$-inch power drill
Circular saw
Saber saw
Hacksaw
Metal file
Router
Level
Framing square

 **MATERIALS**

$\frac{3}{4}$-, $\frac{1}{2}$-, and $\frac{1}{4}$-inch clear birch plywood
$\frac{1}{4}$-inch wood lattice
1-by-2s for cleats
Carpenter's glue
Sandpaper (medium grit)
Shims
Drawer-glide assemblies
$1\frac{5}{8}$-inch trimhead screws
No. 6 finishing nails
No. 8 flathead screws
1-inch wire brads
$1\frac{1}{2}$-inch piano hinge
Magnetic catch

CONSTRUCTING SWING-OUT SHELVES

1. Determining the dimensions.

A swing-out shelf unit *(disassembled at right)* is made of $\frac{3}{4}$-inch birch plywood, with shelf rims of $\frac{1}{4}$-inch lattice. The pieces are held together by glue and $1\frac{5}{8}$-inch trimhead screws.

◆ The height of the unit is 1 to $1\frac{1}{2}$ inches less than the height of the cabinet opening. To ensure swinging clearance, make the width of the unit narrower than the cabinet opening by a third of the unit's depth.

◆ The unit's total depth is the sum of the shelf depths plus the thickness of the partition and shelf rims. In the example shown here, with $3\frac{3}{4}$-inch shelves for standard-size cans, the depth is $8\frac{3}{4}$ inches.

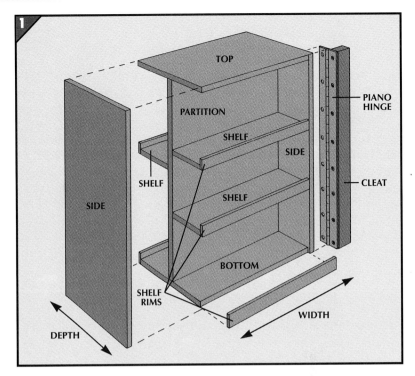

2. Assembling the sides and partition.

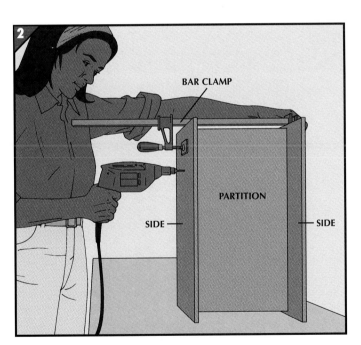

◆ Cut two sides from $\frac{3}{4}$-inch plywood to the planned height and depth of the unit. Cut the partition $1\frac{1}{2}$ inches shorter and narrower than the height and width.

◆ Clamp the partition between the sides so that it is centered top to bottom as well as front to back.

◆ Mark the thickness of the partition on the top edge of each side. Use the marks as guides for pilot holes for $1\frac{5}{8}$-inch trimhead screws at 6- to 8- inch intervals through each side *(above)*.

3. Adding the top and bottom.

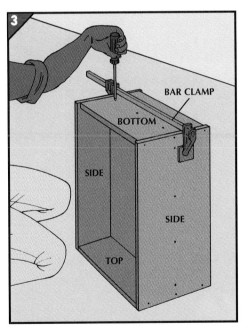

◆ Cut top and bottom pieces $1\frac{1}{2}$ inches shorter than the width of the unit. Match the top piece to the unit's total depth, and make the bottom piece $\frac{1}{2}$ inch narrower to accommodate shelf rims.

◆ Slide the top into position atop the partition; clamp the sides against it. Drill pilot holes for $1\frac{5}{8}$-inch trimhead screws to attach the top piece to the partition and side pieces. Screw the top in place.

◆ Turn the unit upside down and attach the bottom piece in the same way *(above)*, centering it between the sides to leave room for rims.

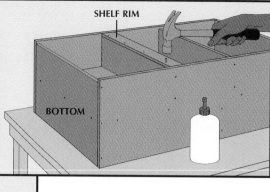

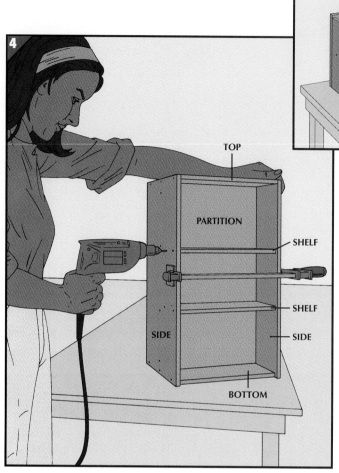

4. Installing the shelves.

◆ Cut shelves as long as the width of the partition and $\frac{1}{4}$ inch narrower than the distance from the partition to the front edge of the side, to leave space for shelf rims.

◆ Position a shelf between the sides, making sure it is level, and clamp the sides to hold it.

◆ Drill two pilot holes through each side into the shelf, placing one about an inch from the front edge of the shelf and the other an inch from the partition *(left)*, and secure the shelf with $1\frac{5}{8}$-inch trimhead screws.

◆ Install the remaining shelves on both sides of the unit in the same way.

◆ Cut a rim for each shelf from $\frac{1}{4}$-inch lattice, as long as the shelf. Apply glue to the front edge of the shelves, and nail the rims flush with the shelf bottoms with 1-inch wire brads *(inset)*.

FINISHING AND INSTALLING THE UNIT

1. Cutting the cabinet shelf.

◆ On each permanent shelf in the cabinet, mark a cutting line parallel to the front edge and as far from the inside of the cabinet frame as the depth of the swing-out unit plus 1 inch. Start the line 1 inch from the same side of the cabinet as the unit's hinge, and make the line several inches longer than the width of the unit, in order to allow swinging clearance. Check these measurements by holding the unit inside the cabinet against the shelf.

◆ Use a saber saw *(left)* or a handsaw to cut the shelf along the line. Smooth the cut edges with medium-grit sandpaper.

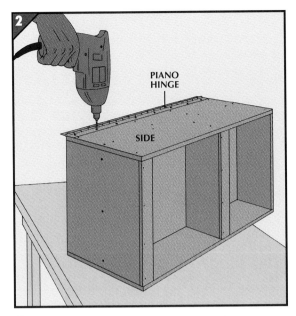

2. Attaching the hinge to the unit.

◆ Position the hinge at the front edge of the pivot side. Center it vertically between the top and bottom and align the hinge barrel with the edge. Drill pilot holes through the screw holes *(above)* and use the screws provided by the manufacturer to attach the hinge.

◆ If the hinge is too long, use a hacksaw to cut it at a joint, but not more than 2 inches shorter than the height of the unit. Smooth the cut edges with a fine metal file.

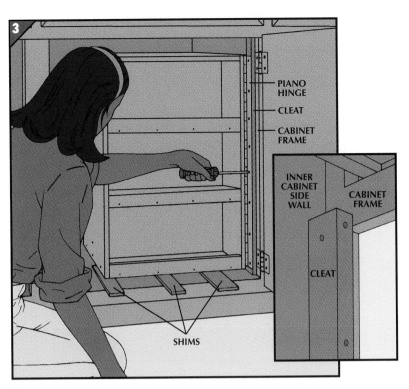

3. Mounting the unit in the cabinet.

◆ Cut a 1-by-2 cleat to the height of the cabinet wall on the pivot side. Attach the cleat to the back of the cabinet frame *(inset)* with $1\frac{5}{8}$-inch trimhead screws driven every 6 to 8 inches through the cleat into the frame.

◆ Drive 3-inch trimhead screws through the side of the cleat and into the cabinet's side wall, at intervals that avoid the screws that are already in place.

◆ Set the unit on shims inside the cabinet and check for swinging clearance at the top.

◆ Position the free hinge leaf on the cleat with the barrel against the cleat's back edge. Mark the hinge holes on the cleat.

◆ Drill pilot holes and use 2-inch No. 4 or No. 5 screws (the largest that will seat flush against the hinge) to secure the hinge to the cleat *(above)*.

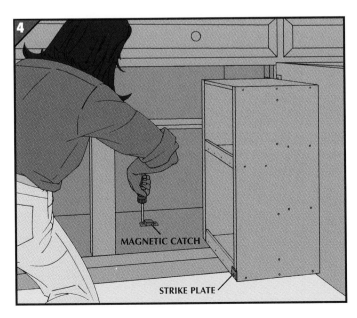

4. Installing the magnetic catch.

◆ Screw the steel strike plate of the catch to the inner bottom corner of the unit on the side away from the hinge. Be sure the edges of the plate are flush with the edges of the corner.

◆ Swing the unit inside the cabinet and position the magnetic catch on the cabinet floor against the strike plate.

◆ Mark the position of screw holes on the cabinet floor, swing the unit out, and use the screws provided with the catch to secure it *(left)*.

DUAL BINS FOR CONVENIENT STORAGE

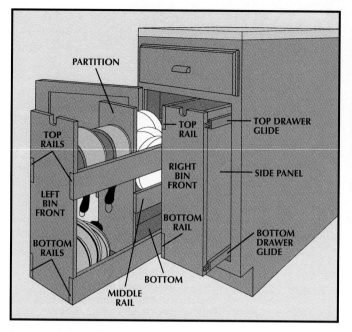

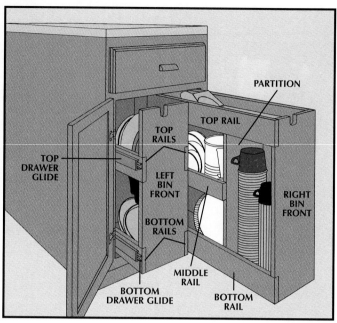

Determining the dimensions.

The overall dimensions of glide-out bins *(above)* allow clearance for sliding and closing the door. The bins are at least 1 inch shorter than the height of the opening and $2\frac{3}{4}$ inches narrower than the width. The depth is $\frac{1}{4}$ inch less than the distance from the back of the cabinet to the inside edge of the front frame. Individual parts, including the width of each bin, are sized according to use.

The bins are made of clear birch plywood: $\frac{3}{4}$ inch for the fronts, backs, and partitions; $\frac{1}{4}$ inch for the side panel, and $\frac{1}{2}$ inch for other parts.

CUTTING THE MAJOR PIECES

Grooved right bin components.

Start by making the front, back, and partition, as well as the rails.

◆ The front and back are as high and wide as the bin; the partition is $3\frac{1}{4}$ inches shorter and $\frac{3}{4}$ inch narrower. The 3-inch-wide top and bottom rails are as long as the unit's depth; the length of the 2-inch-wide middle rail is determined by the position of the partition *(Step 2, page 84)*.

◆ A routed notch 1 inch wide and $\frac{3}{4}$ inch deep at the top front serves as a pull. Corner cutouts sawed in the front and back are 3 inches by $\frac{1}{2}$ inch; a middle cutout in the back is 2 inches wide.

◆ Dadoes $\frac{1}{2}$ inch wide and $\frac{1}{4}$ inch deep across the top of the front and back and in the top rail form a continuous groove after assembly; so do dadoes at the bottom of the front and back and in the bottom rail. A dado $\frac{1}{4}$ inch from the bottom of the middle cutout aligns with dadoes across the partition and in the middle rail. A rabbet $\frac{1}{4}$ inch wide and $\frac{1}{4}$ inch deep on the right edge of the front and back fits the side panel.

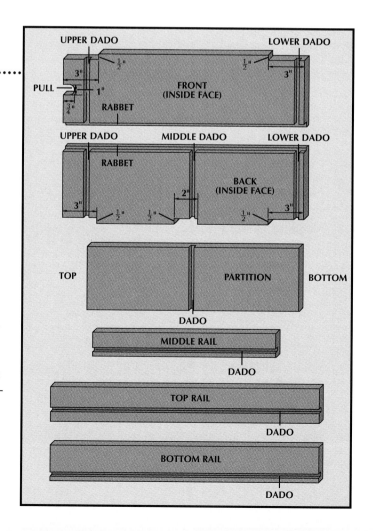

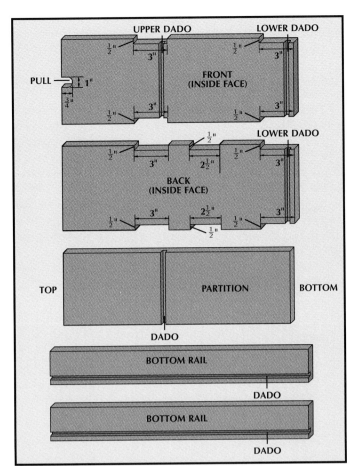

Grooved left bin components.

As with the right bin, make the front, back, and partition. Cut the bottom rails, but make the top and middle rails once the partition is in place *(page 87)*.

◆ The front and back are the planned height and width of the bin, and the partition is $\frac{1}{2}$ inch shorter and 1 inch narrower. Two 3-inch-wide bottom rails are as long as the unit's depth.

◆ The upper cutouts on the front and back are positioned to allow room for planned storage, as are the middle cutouts on the back. The upper and bottom corner cutouts are 3 inches by $\frac{1}{2}$ inch, and the middle cutout is 2 inches by $\frac{1}{2}$ inch.

◆ A notch routed at the top front serves as a pull. A $\frac{1}{2}$-inch-wide dado cut $\frac{1}{4}$ inch deep across the front is $\frac{1}{4}$ inch from the bottom of the upper cutout; the partition's dado aligns with it. The lower dadoes on the front and back are $\frac{1}{4}$ inch above the bottom, as are the dadoes running the length of the bottom rails.

Straight Cuts with a Router

A router makes fast work of the precise cuts crucial to cabinet joints. The variety of available bits and the router's adjustable cutting depth allow cuts of almost any size or shape. A rabbeting bit *(photograph, far right)*, which cuts a notch on the edge of a board, usually has a ball-bearing guide on its tip that rides along the edge, keeping the cut at a uniform width. A straight bit *(photograph, bottom right)*, which makes a square-bottom groove or dado, has no such guide. To ensure straight cuts, clamp a perfectly straight board to the workpiece, parallel to the cutting line and at a distance that allows the bit to just cut the line. Hold the router firmly against the guide when cutting *(right)*. For either type of cut, grip the router with both hands and move it against the resistance of the cutting.

⚠ **CAUTION** *Always wear goggles when routing, and never start the router with the bit in contact with the workpiece.*

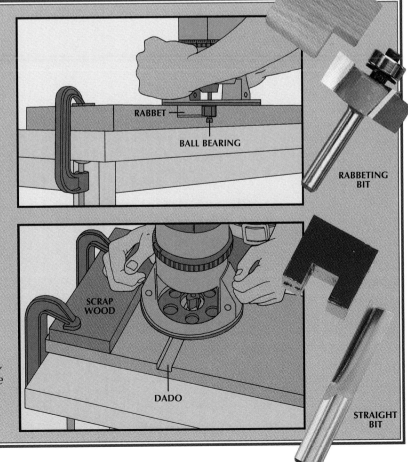

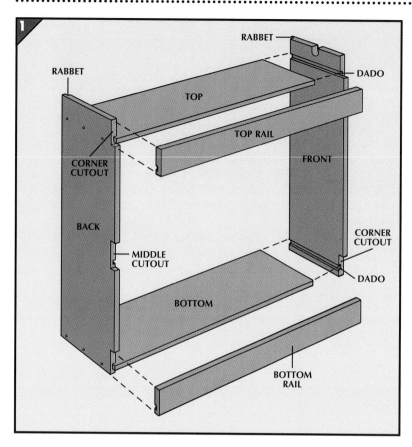

1. Building the frame.

◆ Cut top and bottom pieces from $\frac{1}{2}$-inch plywood, 1 inch shorter than the depth of the cabinet and $\frac{1}{2}$ inch narrower than the front and back.

◆ Apply glue to both ends of the top and bottom and slip them into the dadoes on the front and back, positioned so that one edge extends $\frac{1}{4}$ inch into the cutouts while the other edge is flush with the inner face of the rabbets.

◆ Clamp the pieces together, and drill three pilot holes through the front and back into the top and bottom. Secure these joints with trimhead screws.

◆ When the glue has set, remove the clamps. Apply glue to the long edges of the top and bottom and slip the dadoes of the top and bottom rails over the edges. Drill pilot holes through the rail ends into the edges of the front and back panels and through the rails into the edges of the top and bottom. Secure the rails with trimhead screws.

2. Constructing the middle shelf.

◆ Cut a shelf from $\frac{1}{2}$-inch plywood, $\frac{1}{4}$ inch wider than the partition and $\frac{1}{2}$ inch longer than the distance from the back to the planned partition location.

◆ Apply glue to one end of the shelf and slip it into the dado on the partition so that the shelf edge on the open side extends $\frac{1}{4}$ inch beyond the partition. Drill pilot holes and secure the joint with trimhead screws through the partition into the shelf.

◆ When the glue is dry, apply glue to the other end of the shelf and to the top and bottom of the partition, and position the assembly in the bin with one side of the shelf extending $\frac{1}{4}$ inch into the middle cutout, and the other side flush with the inner face of the rabbets. Complete the joints with screws through the back, top, bottom, and rails.

◆ Glue and screw the middle rail to the protruding edge of the shelf.

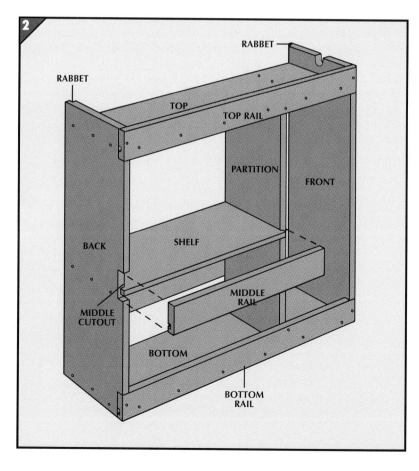

3. Attaching the side panel and sliding channels.

◆ Cut the side panel from $\frac{1}{4}$-inch plywood, to fit snugly within the rabbets.

◆ Position the panel in the rabbets and use a pencil to outline the edges of the top, bottom, shelf, and partition on the panel. Transfer the outlines to the other side of the panel, and reposition it with these marks facing up.

◆ Place the glide channels on the panel, with their front ends flush with the front of the bin and their mounting screw holes centered over the outlines of the top and bottom. Mark the screw holes.

◆ Glue the side panel to the bin and secure it with No. 6 finishing nails countersunk along all the outlines, taking care to avoid the marked screw positions.

◆ Align the top sliding channel with the screw hole markings, and attach it with the screws provided, driven through the panel into the top.

◆ Position the bottom sliding channel over its markings and use a framing square to make sure the distance between the top and bottom channels is equal at both ends *(left)*, then secure the channel with screws through the side panel into the bottom.

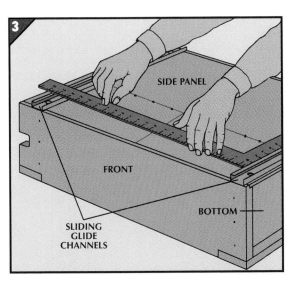

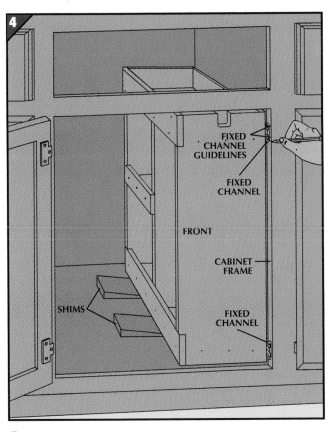

4. Positioning the bin.

◆ Slip the fixed glide channels over the sliding channels on the bin. Position the bin in the cabinet on shims so it is level and clears the top and side of the opening.

◆ Mark the locations of the upper and lower fixed channels on the edge of the cabinet frame *(above)*.

◆ Measure the distance between the fixed channels and the cabinet wall. Use 1-by-2 clear pine to make two mounting cleats of that thickness and as long as the cabinet depth.

5. Installing the bin.

◆ Extend lines from the marks on the cabinet edge along the sides and 1 inch onto the back of the cabinet.

◆ Position a fixed channel against a cleat, flush with the front edge, and drill mounting holes in the cleat.

◆ Center a cleat on the upper guidelines, and avoiding the mounting holes, drill four pilot holes through the cleat into the side wall. Attach the cleat with No. 8 screws *(above)*.

◆ Mount the lower cleat the same way.

◆ Screw the fixed channels to the cleats using longer screws than those provided, for added strength.

◆ Install the bin by inserting the sliding channels into the cabinet-mounted fixed channels.

ASSEMBLING THE LEFT BIN

1. Making the bottom.

◆ Cut a bottom piece 1 inch shorter than the depth of the cabinet, and $\frac{1}{2}$ inch narrower than the front and back.

◆ Apply glue to the ends of the bottom piece and slip it into the lower dadoes on the front and back, with its edges extending $\frac{1}{4}$ inch into the cutouts on both sides. Clamp the bottom in place, drill pilot holes into its edge through the front and back, and secure it with trimhead screws.

◆ Apply glue to the edges of the bottom, then attach the two bottom rails with screws into the bottom on the front and back.

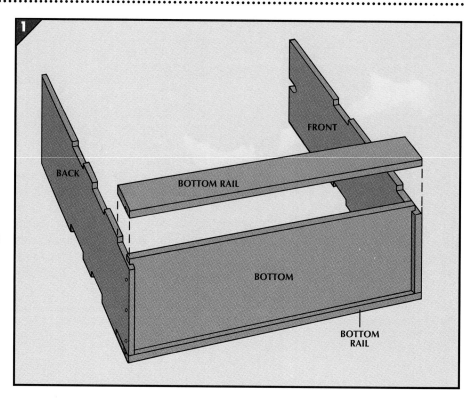

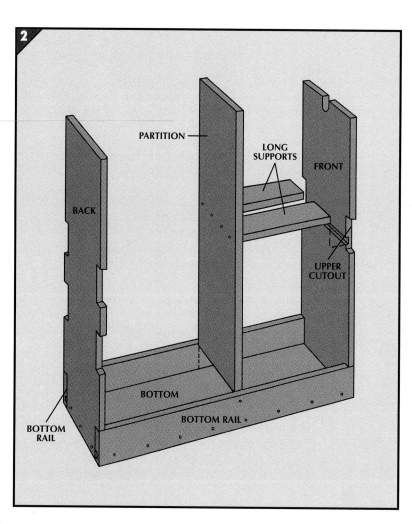

2. Building the long supports.

◆ Cut long supports *(left)* from $\frac{1}{2}$-inch plywood to the length corresponding to the planned position of the partition, adding $\frac{1}{2}$ inch to allow for the dadoes. Make each support wide enough to leave a gap between them for pot handles when their outer edges are flush with the edge of the partition.

◆ Apply glue to one end of each support and slip them into the partition dado, outer edges flush with the edges of the partition. Clamp the pieces together, drill pilot holes through the partition, and secure the pieces with trimhead screws.

◆ Apply glue to the free ends of the supports and the bottom of the partition, then set the assembly in the bin with the supports fitted firmly into the front dado.

◆ Secure the assembly with screws through the front, bottom, and rails.

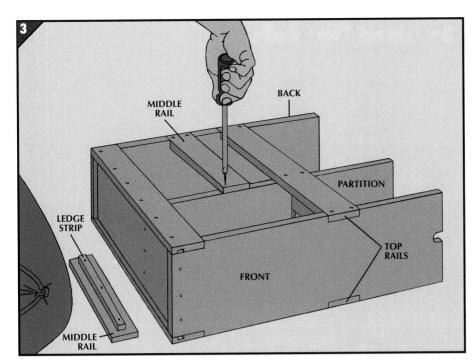

3. Constructing the top and middle rails.

◆ Make two top rails with the same dimensions as the bottom rails. Glue and screw them into the upper cutouts on the front and back.

◆ Make two middle rails $2\frac{1}{2}$ inches wide and as long as the distance from the outside of the back piece to the front side of the partition.

◆ Cut two ledge strips, $1\frac{1}{2}$ inches shorter than the middle rails and $\frac{3}{4}$ inch wide, and center one on each middle rail. Secure them with glue and trimhead screws.

◆ With the ledge strips facing inward, glue and screw the middle rails to the partition and the middle cutouts on the back (*left*).

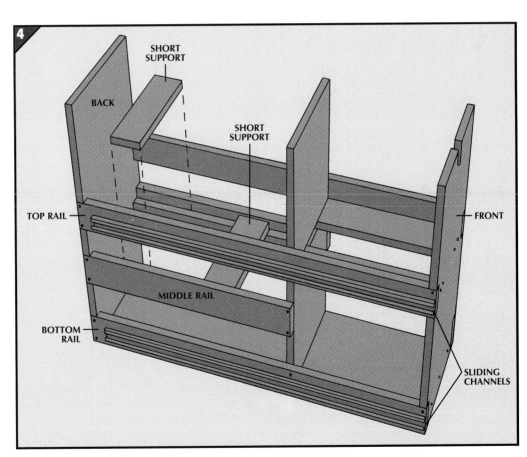

4. Completing the left bin.

◆ Make two short supports as long as the distance between the inside edges of the middle rails. Their width can vary, but they must be wide enough to support the smallest item you plan to store.

◆ Lower the short supports onto the ledge strips and leave them loose or glue them.

◆ Attach the sliding channels to the top and bottom rails of the bin, centered and flush with the front, and mount the bin in the cabinet (*page 85*).

An Island That Rolls

Four swivel casters and a butcher-block top can transform a pair of kitchen cabinets into a movable island. With the cabinets fastened back to back, this unit offers additional storage space with adjustable shelves and doors on opposite sides, plus an extra work surface that goes where you need it.

Buy two preassembled wall cabinets, 12 inches deep and anywhere from 18 to 60 inches wide, depending on your needs and the size of your kitchen. To make the island the same height as your countertop—typically 36 inches—choose cabinets 30 inches high; the swivel casters and butcher-block top will add the rest. The top should overhang the cabinets on all four sides by 3 inches, providing handholds for rolling the island. Select cabinets with tops and bottoms of plywood or particle board at least $\frac{1}{2}$ inch thick and add solid wood reinforcing boards to support the casters and butcher block.

If the joint where the two cabinets fit together is noticeable, fill it with wood putty or conceal it under $1\frac{1}{4}$- by $\frac{1}{4}$-inch wood lath, fastened with carpenter's glue and countersunk brads.

TOOLS

$\frac{3}{8}$-inch power drill
Circular saw
Awl
Medium-size flat-blade
    screwdriver
Adjustable wrench

MATERIALS

Two matching kitchen wall
    cabinets
Laminated maple butcher
    block, at least $1\frac{3}{4}$ inches
    thick
Four 1-by-8 pine or fir boards
Four flat-plate locking swivel
    casters, with $2\frac{1}{2}$-inch wheels
    and 75-lb. load capacity
    rating

Six $\frac{1}{4}$- by 3-inch stove bolts,
    each with 1 nut, 2 flat wash-
    ers, and 1 split lock washer
Eight No. 8 $1\frac{1}{4}$-inch round-
    head wood screws
Sixteen No. 8 $\frac{3}{4}$-inch round-
    head wood screws
Six No. 10 3-inch round-head
    wood screws, each with 1
    flat washer

JOINING TWO CABINETS

1. Drilling holes for bolts.

◆ Remove the doors and shelves from the cabinets and lay them facedown, tops facing each other and sides flush.
◆ With a pencil, mark $\frac{1}{2}$ inch down from the top edge and 2 inches in from each side of the cabinets. Make a third mark halfway between.
◆ Make sure the marks on both cabinets align with each other, then turn the cabinets around and repeat along the bottoms.
◆ Drill $\frac{1}{4}$-inch holes through the lip of the recessed area at each mark (*left*).

2. Bolting cabinets together.

◆ Set the cabinets upright, back to back, and push an awl through each pair of holes to align them. Slide flat washers onto three stove bolts, and push each bolt through the holes in both cabinets. Put a flat washer and a split washer on each bolt, followed by a nut; then turn each nut finger tight.

◆ Turn the cabinets over by tipping them on their sides, not on a front panel. Bolt the bottom edges together the same way as the top. After all six bolts are in place, hold each bolthead with a screwdriver and tighten the nut with a wrench until the split lock washer is compressed.

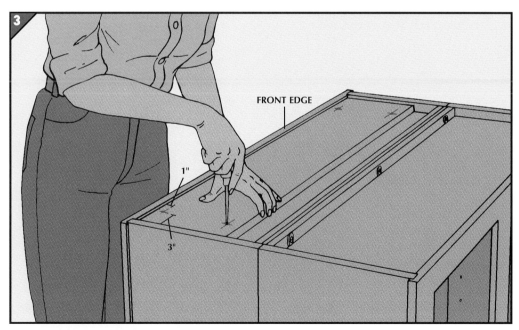

3. Fitting the reinforcement boards.

◆ Measure the length of the recessed area on the cabinet tops and bottoms and cut four pieces of 1-by-8 to that length.

◆ Make four marks on each board, 3 inches from the ends and 1 inch from the edges, and drill $\frac{3}{32}$-inch holes at each mark.

◆ Set a board in one of the cabinet recess-es, snug against the front edge of the cabinet. Insert an awl into each hole in the board and push the point firmly into the cabinet (*above*). Remove the board, and drill a $\frac{3}{16}$-inch hole through the cabinet at each awl mark. Repeat the process for each reinforcement board in each of the remaining three recesses.

4. Fastening the boards to the cabinets.

◆ Set one of the reinforcement boards into its cabinet recess and push the awl through the holes to align them.

◆ Then, reach inside the cabinet and drive a $1\frac{1}{4}$-inch No. 8 wood screw through each hole in the cabinet and up into the board (*below*). Install the remaining reinforcement boards the same way.

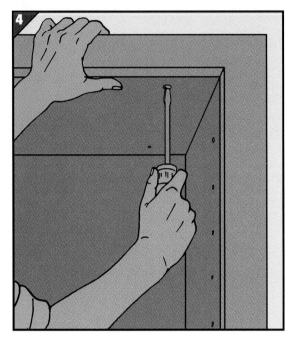

5. Attaching the casters.

◆ Turn the cabinets bottom side up. Set a caster in each corner with the holes in the mounting plate at least $\frac{1}{2}$ inch from the edges of the reinforcement board. Mark the board through the holes in the plate.

◆ With a $\frac{3}{32}$-inch bit, drill $\frac{3}{4}$-inch-deep pilot holes (*page 10*) at each mark. Fasten the casters to the board with $\frac{3}{4}$-inch No. 8 wood screws.

◆ Unfinished cabinets—including the doors and shelves—should be painted or stained before proceeding to the next step.

MOUNTING A BUTCHER-BLOCK TOP

1. Drilling through cabinet roof.

◆ Turn the cabinets upright again, then measure and mark 2 inches in from each side and 1 inch back from the front edge of the reinforcement boards. Center a third mark between these two.

◆ Drill $\frac{1}{4}$-inch holes through the reinforcement boards and the cabinet tops at each mark.

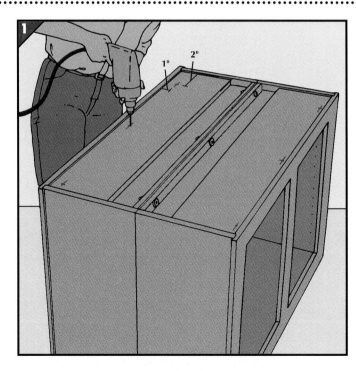

2. Marking the butcher block.

Set the butcher block upside down and, with a straightedge, draw a line 3 inches in from and parallel to each edge. Affix two pieces of masking tape at each corner as shown above, aligning the inner edges of the tape with the lines.

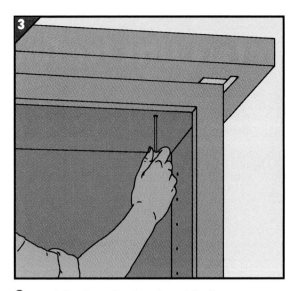

3. Positioning the butcher block.

◆ Set the butcher block on the cabinets, aligning the tape strips with the cabinet corners. Push an awl through each hole in the cabinet roof to mark the underside of the butcher block.

◆ Remove the butcher block and turn it over. Then, with a $\frac{1}{8}$-inch bit, drill $\frac{1}{2}$-inch-deep pilot holes at each mark.

4. Attaching the butcher block.

◆ Reposition the butcher block on the cabinet. With the awl, align the holes in the cabinet roof with those in the block.

◆ Slip flat washers onto six 3-inch No. 10 wood screws, and drive the screws partway into the block. When all the screws are in place, go back and tighten each one completely.

◆ Remove the masking tape. Replace the shelves and rehang the doors.

Face-Lifts for Timeworn Kitchens

You can bring an old-fashioned kitchen up to date by building on what you already have. Modern amenities such as soap dispensers and water filters are easy to add, as is a new countertop in a fresh color. Instead of replacing old cabinets, consider sprucing them up with new doors, drawer fronts, and matching veneer for the frames. Very often, a new floor can be installed right over the old one.

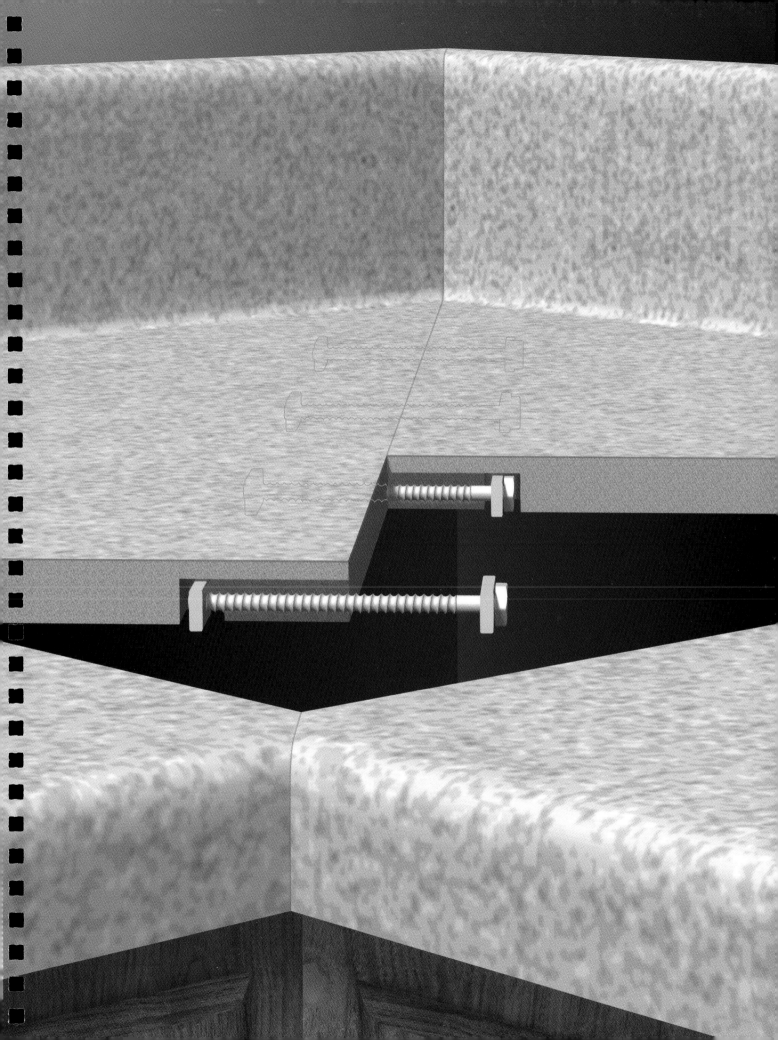

A Safer Electrical Receptacle

Since the mid-1970s, the National Electrical Code has required that any electrical receptacle that is installed within 6 feet of a sink must be protected by a ground-fault circuit interrupter, or GFCI. This device detects the smallest leakage of electrical current—called a ground fault—and turns off power in the receptacle within $\frac{1}{40}$ second.

Replacing an old receptacle with a new GFCI is economical insurance. Because one GFCI protects all receptacles that are downstream from it on the same circuit, you can install the device anywhere on the kitchen circuit between the service panel and the receptacles that require this protection.

For a GFCI to function, the wires must be properly connected to the terminals labeled "line" and "load." Reversing these connections will still allow electricity to flow through the receptacle, but it will render the GFCI protection inoperative.

Before Proceeding: Some jurisdictions require a permit for any work on a house's electrical wiring and an inspection once it's completed. Also check your house for aluminum wiring; it is dull gray in color, sometimes coated with copper. The code allows only specially licensed electricians to work on it. If you have any doubts, consult an electrician.

> ⚠️ **CAUTION** *First, trip the circuit breaker or unscrew the fuse in the service panel that protects the receptacle's circuit. Then remove the cover plate and set a multitester for 250 volts AC. Touch one probe to the green grounding screw and the other in turn to each silver- and brass-colored screw. Repeat the test at the 10-volt AC setting. Any reading other than 0 volts indicates that there is a problem in the circuit; call an electrician.*

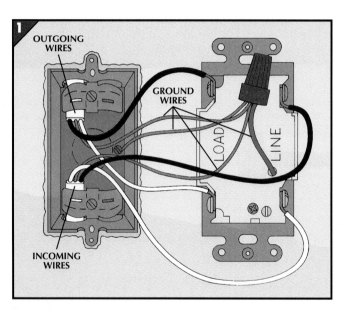

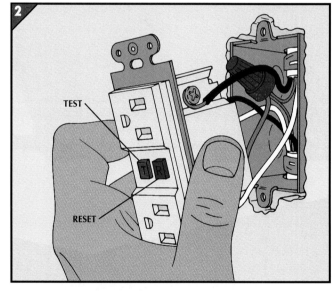

1. Wiring the GFCI.

◆ With the power off, remove the receptacle and disconnect the bottom set of black and white wires. Plug a radio into the receptacle and turn the power back on; if the radio is silent, you have disconnected the incoming wires.
◆ Turn off power at the service panel. Attach incoming wires to the "line" side of the GFCI, black to the brass-colored screw post and white to the silver-colored post. Connect outgoing wires to the "load" side of the GFCI, black to brass and white to silver. Attach a short length of bare copper wire to the box's green screw post. Use a wire cap to join this wire with all other green or bare copper wires in the box and the GFCI *(above).*
◆ Some GFCIs have wire leads instead of screws. Proceed as instructed above, but match wires by color and connect them with wire caps.

2. Mounting the GFCI.

◆ Tuck the wires back into the electrical box, then secure the GFCI receptacle to the box with the mounting screws and replace the cover plate.
◆ Turn on power at the service panel and test the GFCI and any protected receptacles between it and the end of the circuit. To do so, plug a radio into each receptacle in turn and push the test button on the GFCI. If in each case the reset button pops out and the radio goes silent, all is well. If the radio does not go off, or if you cannot push the reset button to restore power, turn off power at the service panel and check the wiring of the GFCI.
◆ If the wiring is correct and the problem persists, either the GFCI is faulty or there is a problem elsewhere. If replacing the GFCI doesn't work, call an electrician.

Soap and hot water at your fingertips, pure water for drinking and cooking, a seemingly endless supply of ice, and bright, glare-free light on a kitchen countertop—any of these add to the efficiency and convenience of a kitchen.

Soap and Hot Water: A soap dispenser and a tap that delivers near-boiling water are usually mounted to a stainless steel sink through a hole cut in the back rim of the sink with a knockout punch *(page 96)*. Piercing the rim of a cast-iron or porcelain sink is impracticable, but either device may be installed in the countertop, provided the soap dispenser or waterspout is long enough to reach the basin.

Installing a hot-water tap requires not only the existence of a new, GFCI-protected receptacle *(page 94)* for an uninterrupted flow of electricity, but also the proximity of a cold-water line that can be tapped. For this purpose, use a saddle valve *(page 98)*, an ingenious, virtually foolproof device for drawing water from copper or plastic pipe. Buy a valve that fits your supply pipes and the flexible tubing for the tap.

Clean Water: Under-the-counter water filters fit into the cold-water line supplying the kitchen sink. The replaceable cartridges in some filters trap sediment, particulate matter, and unpleasant tastes found in water, while others remove lead, chemicals, and bacteria.

Ice on Tap: Almost all models of refrigerators made since the early 1970s allow for the installation of an icemaker, usually obtained from the manufacturer as a kit.

The icemaker must be connected to a cold-water-supply pipe by $\frac{1}{4}$-inch copper tubing. Use a saddle valve to tap into a water pipe convenient for routing the tubing to the back of the refrigerator.

Under-Cabinet Lighting: A fluorescent light mounted under a cabinet provides bright, glare-free illumination for a countertop or sink.

Home-improvement stores sell ready-to-install lighting that can be plugged into any handy receptacle.

TOOLS

Center punch or nail set	Adjustable wrench
Knockout punch	Open-end wrench
Basin wrench	Wire stripper
Hacksaw or tube cutter	Wirecutters
Pipe reamer	Drill
Emery board	Utility knife
Torpedo level	Screwdriver or nut driver

MATERIALS

Plumber's putty	Compression fittings
Plumbing tape	Insulated wire
Saddle valve	staples
$\frac{1}{4}$-inch flexible copper tubing	$\frac{3}{8}$-inch wood screws

MOUNTING A SOAP DISPENSER AT THE SINK

1. Drilling a starter hole.
◆ Pick a location on the back rim of the sink where there is sufficient space underneath for the soap reservoir.
◆ Mark a point on the rim so that the pump flange *(far right)* rests fully on metal and does not overhang the sink or extend over the countertop. Dimple the rim at that point with a center punch or nail set *(right)*.
◆ Drill a starter hole at the dimple with a $\frac{1}{8}$-inch bit. Then widen the hole to $\frac{7}{16}$ inch with increasingly larger bits.

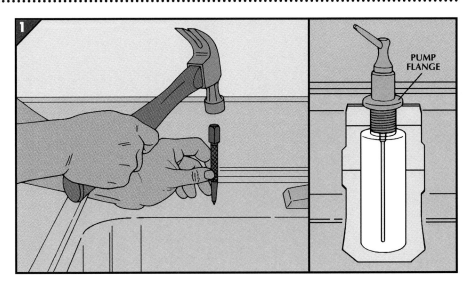

PUMP FLANGE

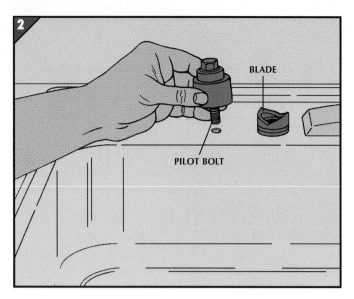

2. Finishing the hole.

◆ Insert the pilot bolt of a knockout punch into the starter hole from the top *(left)*. From beneath the sink, screw the bladed part of the tool onto the bolt hand tight.

◆ Turn the bolt with a wrench until the blade cuts through the stainless steel. To avoid bruised knuckles as the punch breaks through, never push the wrench handle away from you; instead, always pull it toward you.

The Knockout Punch

This ingenious tool cuts precise holes in stainless steel quickly and easily. A bolt, passed through a pilot hole drilled in the metal, connects the top and bottom halves of the punch. Turning the bolt head at the top pulls the bottom—with its finely honed cutting edge—upward through the steel. Most tool-rental stores carry a selection of knockout punches in diameters from $\frac{1}{2}$ inch to as large as $4\frac{1}{2}$ inches, usually in $\frac{1}{8}$-inch increments.

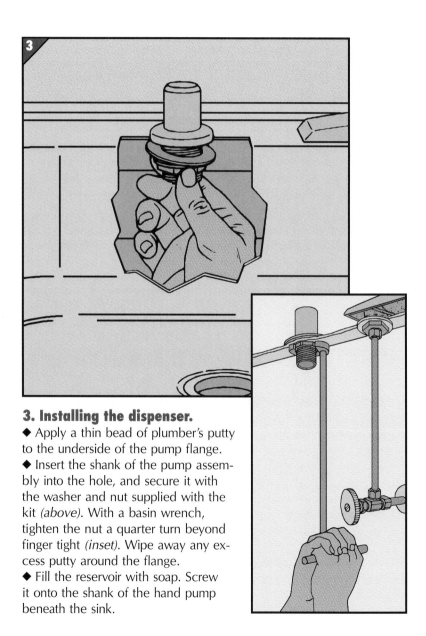

3. Installing the dispenser.

◆ Apply a thin bead of plumber's putty to the underside of the pump flange.

◆ Insert the shank of the pump assembly into the hole, and secure it with the washer and nut supplied with the kit *(above)*. With a basin wrench, tighten the nut a quarter turn beyond finger tight *(inset)*. Wipe away any excess putty around the flange.

◆ Fill the reservoir with soap. Screw it onto the shank of the hand pump beneath the sink.

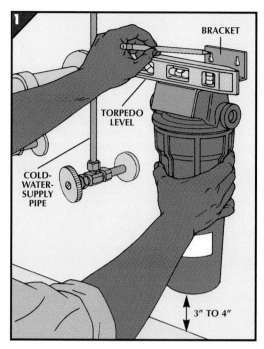

1. Attaching the mounting bracket.

◆ Place the filter housing on the mounting bracket. Choose a location for the bracket to the right of the cold-water-supply pipe leading to the faucet. Also allow 3 to 4 inches above the floor for clearance when changing filter cartridges.

◆ Hold the bracket level against the wall, and mark the holes for mounting screws *(above)*.

◆ Set the bracket aside, and drive the screws into the back of the cabinet, leaving about $\frac{1}{4}$ inch of each screw exposed.

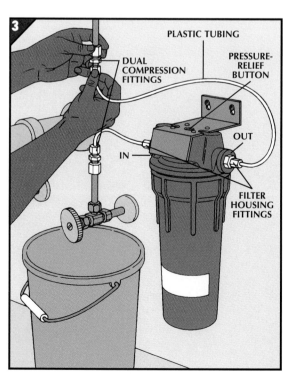

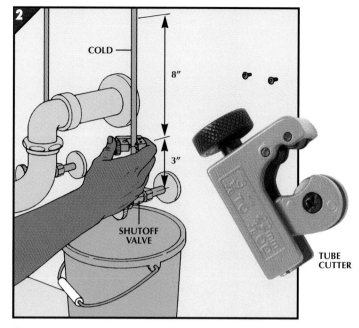

2. Attaching the fittings.

◆ Close the cold-water shutoff valve, then mark the cold-water pipe 3 inches above the valve and 8 inches above that mark.

◆ Place a bucket below the pipe to catch drips, then cut out the piece of pipe between the marks with a tube cutter *(above)* or hacksaw.

◆ Smooth the pipe edges on both sides of the gap with an emery board, and clean out the cut ends with a pipe reamer. Then slip one of the dual compression fittings that come with the filter kit over each end of the cut pipe. To avoid damaging the compression rings, tighten each fitting only one turn past hand tight with an adjustable wrench.

◆ Working in a clockwise direction, wrap two layers of plumbing tape around the threads of the fittings that screw into the in and out ports of the filter housing. Screw the fittings into the ports, and tighten one turn past hand tight.

3. Hooking up the filter.

◆ Shorten the flexible plastic tubes so that they reach from the dual compression fittings on the pipe to the in and out ports of the filter without being either too long or so short that they curve sharply.

◆ Insert a length of plastic tubing in the dual fitting coming from the shutoff valve, and connect it to the threaded fitting occupying the in port of the filter housing. Fasten another tube to the fitting in the out port, and connect it to the upper dual fitting on the pipe.

◆ Hang the bracket on the mounting screws and tighten them. Open the cold-water shutoff valve and press the pressure-relief button on the filter to release air displaced as water enters. Tighten any leaky fittings by a quarter turn until the seepage stops.

◆ Run cold water from the tap for 2 or 3 minutes, both to saturate the filter cartridge and to flush out loose material.

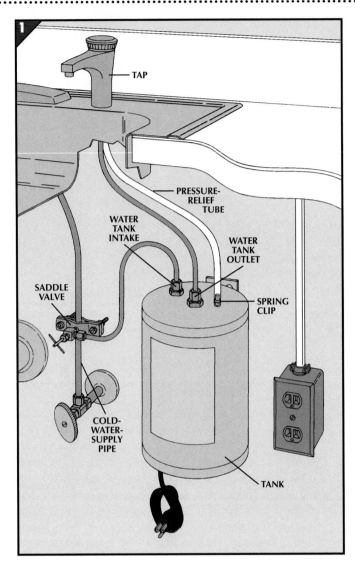

TAP

PRESSURE-RELIEF TUBE

WATER TANK INTAKE

WATER TANK OUTLET

SADDLE VALVE

SPRING CLIP

COLD-WATER-SUPPLY PIPE

TANK

1. Mounting the tap and tank.

◆ Choose a location for the tap on the sink rim where the spout will overhang the sink. Then cut a hole in the rim with a knockout punch as shown on page 96.

◆ Lay a thin bead of plumber's putty around the tap's flange, or use the gasket supplied with some kits. Insert the shank of the tap in the hole. Secure it with the washer and lock nut supplied with the unit, and tighten gently with a basin wrench *(page 96)*. Some models use bolts and a metal brace to hold the tap from the underside of the sink rim.

◆ Below the sink, level the mounting bracket for the water heater tank, and screw it to the inside cabinet wall as close as possible to the cold-water-supply pipe. Mount the tank onto the bracket.

⚠ **CAUTION** *The water tank gets hot; rags or flammable substances should not be stored in the same cabinet.*

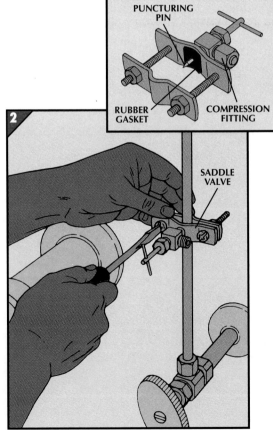

PUNCTURING PIN

RUBBER GASKET

COMPRESSION FITTING

SADDLE VALVE

2. Tapping a water line.

◆ Close the shutoff valve to the cold-water-supply pipe.

◆ Turn the handle of the saddle valve counterclockwise until the puncturing pin is fully recessed beneath the rubber gasket *(inset)*.

◆ Join the two pieces of the valve around the pipe, and draw them together snugly with the nuts and bolts provided *(right)*.

◆ Insert a length of flexible copper tubing into the compression fitting of the saddle valve. To avoid damaging the compression ring inside it, turn the nut one turn past hand tight.

◆ Use a compression fitting to fasten the tubing to the water-tank intake *(above)*. Use copper tubing and compression fittings to connect the tank's outlet port to the underside of the tap.

◆ Attach the pressure-relief tube, which is connected to the tap at the factory, to the small brass nipple at the top of the tank, and secure it with the spring clip supplied with the kit.

◆ Open the cold-water shutoff. Turn the handle of the saddle valve clockwise until the pin punctures the pipe, then open the valve to adjust water flow. Check for leaks, and tighten fittings as needed.

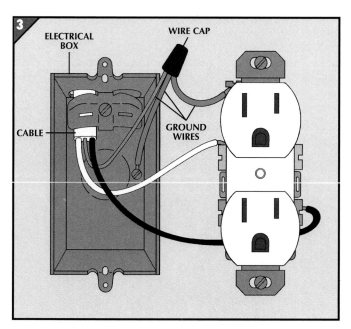

ELECTRICAL BOX WIRE CAP

CABLE GROUND WIRES

3. Wiring a new receptacle.

◆ Extend a 20-amp circuit to a convenient spot below the sink, and install a surface-mounted electrical box there for the new receptacle. If the circuit is not protected by a GFCI, install one (page 94).

◆ Connect the black wire in the cable to one of the brass-colored screws on the receptacle and the white wire to a silver-colored screw. Cut short ground wires for the receptacle and the box, and join them with a wire cap to the bare wire in the cable as shown (left).

◆ Push the receptacle into the box, and secure it with the screws provided. Then install the cover plate.

◆ Plug in the water heater.

AN ICEMAKER FOR THE FREEZER

1. Mounting the icemaker.

◆ Unplug the refrigerator and pull it away from the wall.

◆ Inside the freezer, lift out the removable back panel to expose the end of the internal water-supply line.

◆ Remove the covers from the mounting holes and the power outlet in the freezer wall. Plug in the icemaker, then screw it into the mounting holes so that the supply line overhangs the water basin on the icemaker.

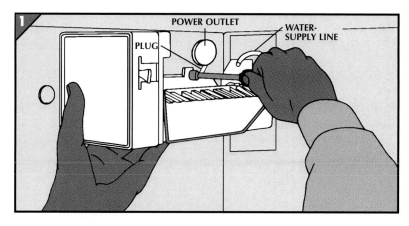

POWER OUTLET WATER-SUPPLY LINE

PLUG

2. Hooking up a water line.

◆ Locate the most convenient cold-water-supply line and close its shutoff valve.

◆ Tap into the line with a saddle valve (page 98). Attach flexible copper tubing to the valve's compression fitting, and run it to the back of the refrigerator. Cut the tubing about 12 inches longer than necessary to reach the water inlet valve.

◆ Slip a compression ring and nut onto the tubing, and insert it in the inlet valve for the icemaker's internal water-supply line (right). The valve can be found at the back of the refrigerator, usually near the floor.

◆ Plug in the refrigerator, turn on the water at the shutoff valve, and open the saddle valve. Check all connections for leaks, and tighten them if necessary.

◆ Adjust the water fill lever and icemaker shutoff arm as described on pages 60 and 61.

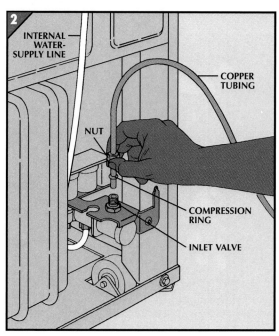

INTERNAL WATER-SUPPLY LINE

COPPER TUBING

NUT

COMPRESSION RING

INLET VALVE

UNDER-CABINET LIGHTING

ELECTRICAL RECEPTACLE

1. Mounting the housing.
◆ Where you choose to install the under-cabinet lighting is a matter of personal taste. The closer it is to the front edge of the cabinet, the more direct light you get on the countertop work area. If it is mounted farther back, the unit itself is hidden from view, but you also get less direct light on the work area.
◆ Hold the housing against the underside of a cabinet and mark the bracket holes, then drill pilot holes $\frac{1}{4}$ inch deep for the mounting screws (page 10).
◆ Attach the fixture housing to the cabinet with wood screws no longer than $\frac{3}{8}$ inch.

2. Attaching the light.
◆ Take the fluorescent bulb out of the light fixture to avoid breaking it as you work.
◆ Secure the fixture to the housing. Some models screw to the housing, others slip into support brackets.

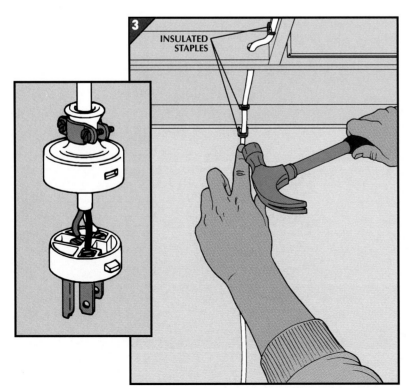

INSULATED STAPLES

3. Hiding the cord.
◆ Run the fixture's cord under the cabinet frame to the nearest grounded wall outlet. Anchor the cord with insulated wire staples every 4 to 6 inches (left).
◆ To overcome an obstacle such as an adjacent cabinet frame, drill a hole through the frame large enough for the cord to pass but not the plug.
◆ If the cord is attached to a plug with screw terminals (inset), take the plug apart, thread the cord through the hole, then reattach the plug. Snip off a molded plug with wirecutters and attach a new grounded plug to the end of the cord.
◆ Install the fluorescent bulb and plug the unit in.

Replacing a Prelaminated Countertop

Replacing an old laminated countertop with a new one can make a quick and dramatic change in the appearance of your kitchen. Aside from the cutting of an opening for the sink, the job consists mostly of simple steps—drilling holes, driving screws, hooking up the sink—and can usually be completed in a single day.

Critical Measurements: The most important element in a smooth installation is the precise measurement of the existing countertop *(below)*. Check your results carefully, and take them, along with a sketch of the counter layout, to the supplier, who will provide the replacement.

Choosing a Style: Available in a wide variety of laminate colors and patterns, countertops also come in

two styles: custom self-edge and postform. The difference lies in the treatment of the front edge and of the joint between the work surface and the backsplash, the short vertical surface that catches overflows and spills at the counter's rear.

In a custom self-edge countertop, the work surface and the backsplash meet in a sharp 90° angle. The front edge is also perpendicular to the work surface. Custom self-edge is the style to choose if you wish to finish the edge with wood trim called bullnose.

A postform counter has a gently rounded front edge and backsplash joint, with the laminate curving smoothly over them. For the neatest job whichever style you choose, specify that the countertop ends, even those that abut a wall or appliance, be covered with laminate.

TOOLS

Tape measure	Utility knife
Basin wrench	Flashlight
Open-end	Drill
wrenches	Saber saw
Screwdriver	Caulk gun

MATERIALS

Prelaminated count-	Masking tape
ertop segments	(2-inch)
Corner fasteners	Utility handle
2-by-2s	Silicone caulk
Roll of paper	Denatured alcohol
(25-inch-wide)	

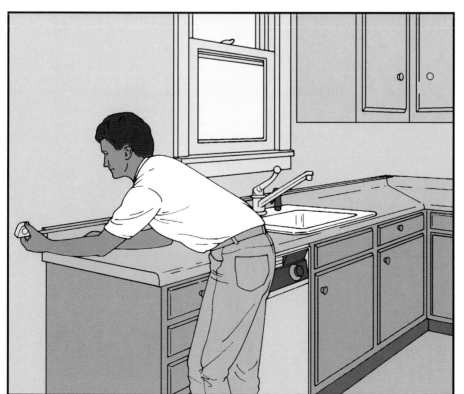

Taking the measurements.
◆ First, measure the length of the countertop. For an L-shaped counter *(left)*, hook the end of a tape measure over the backsplash and measure the length of each leg of the old countertop.
◆ Check the distance from the back of the backsplash to the front edge. If the distance differs from the standard 25 inches, specify the actual measurement when ordering the replacement.

1. Removing the sink.

◆ Turn off the water supply to the faucet. Open the faucet to drain the supply lines, then disconnect them from the faucet with a basin wrench. Use the same tool to remove the dishwasher air gap *(page 32)*.

◆ Cut power to the dishwasher and garbage disposer at the service panel. Disconnect drain and dishwasher plumbing from the disposer, then detach it from the sink *(left)*, either by turning it to unlock it or by loosening mounting screws under the sink. Set the disposer on the cabinet floor.

◆ Unscrew the anchors under the countertop that hold the sink. Separate the countertop and the sink edge with a utility knife, then lift out the sink and set it aside.

2. Making a sink template.

◆ Cut a sheet of paper long enough to extend from one end of the countertop past the sink cutout. Tape the paper even with the end of the countertop and with one edge against the backsplash. Mark these edges of the paper *(Xs)*.

◆ Using the corners of the sink cutout as guides, cut through the paper with a utility knife to make an opening at each corner *(right)*.

CORNER OPENING

3. Removing the old countertop.

◆ Using a flashlight to illuminate the dark corners, examine cabinet corner braces for screws in the underside of the countertop. Remove any screws you find and save them for securing the new countertop.

◆ Remove the screws that secure the dishwasher to the underside of the countertop.

◆ If the space between the backsplash and the wall is filled with caulk, cut the caulk away with a utility knife.

◆ With a helper, lift the old countertop from the cabinets.

CORNER BRACE

INSTALLING THE NEW COUNTERTOP

1. Marking a sink cutout.
◆ Cut 2-by-2s to support the new countertop when marking and cutting the sink opening. With a helper, set the countertop on the supports.
◆ Tape the template to the countertop using the marks that were made earlier to position it.
◆ With a marker, transfer the corners cut into the template to the countertop *(left)*. Remove the template and join the corners with the marker and a straightedge.
◆ Cover the resulting outline of the sink cutout with strips of 2-inch-wide masking tape to protect the laminate when you saw it. If the cutting line is not visible through the tape, remove the tape and darken the line, then re-place the tape.

2. Cutting the sink opening.
◆ Screw a handle to the countertop in the center of the cutout, then drill a 1-inch-diameter hole inside the cutout area, near a corner.
◆ Fit a blade suitable for cutting laminate into a saber saw. Start the saw with the blade in the hole and cut toward the line, then along it *(left)*.
◆ As you approach the end of the cut, grasp the handle to prevent the waste piece from sagging, which might split the laminate.

3. Positioning the countertop.
◆ While you lift the countertop slightly at the sink cutout, have a helper slide out the front 2-by-2 support, followed by the rear support *(above)*.
◆ For an L-shaped cabinet, lift the other countertop section onto the cabinet to help align both pieces while you finish installing the first one.
◆ Set the sink in the cutout, adjusting sink and countertop so that the sink drain aligns with the drainpipe in the wall and the backsplash fits against the wall.

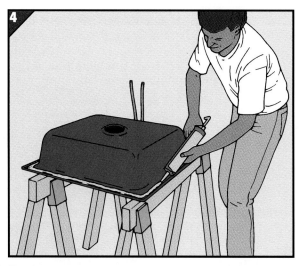

4. Caulking the sink.
◆ Pencil a line perpendicular to the front edge of the sink and continue it onto the countertop to mark the sink position. Draw a similar line at one edge of the sink, then remove the sink and support it upside down above the floor.
◆ Clean any old caulk from the underside of the sink, then apply a thin bead of caulk around the outer edge of the sink lip *(above)*.
◆ Apply a $\frac{1}{4}$-inch-thick bead of caulk to the countertop around the edge of the sink cutout.

5. Reinstalling the sink.
◆ To avoid disturbing the fresh caulk, lift the sink by the base of the faucet and the drain hole.
◆ Set the sink into the cutout, aligning the pencil marks on the sink edges with those on the countertop.
◆ Reconnect all plumbing detached during removal of the sink.
◆ Screw in the anchors that hold the sink in place, drilling pilot holes for the screws if necessary.
◆ Wipe excess caulk from around the sink edge with a rag dampened with denatured alcohol.

6. Securing the countertop.

◆ To bore pilot holes for the anchoring screws from the old countertop, use a drill bit slightly narrower than the screws. Prevent the bit from going all the way through the countertop by wrapping the bit with tape. Place the tape at a distance from the drill tip equal to the screw length less $\frac{1}{8}$ inch.

◆ Drill pilot holes through the existing holes in the cabinet corner braces as shown at left. (Pilot holes need not be vertical.) Screw the countertop in place.

◆ Screw the dishwasher to the underside of the countertop.

7. Completing an L-shaped countertop.

◆ Slide the unfastened section along the cabinet and apply a thin bead of caulk to the mitered edge. Then slip the sections together again.

◆ Insert a corner fastener—a bolt with a rectangular nut and washer—in each of the channels precut at the joint. With a helper to hold the countertop sections flush with each other, tighten the fasteners with a wrench, back to front *(right)*. Wipe excess caulk from the joint.

◆ Screw the countertop to the cabinet.

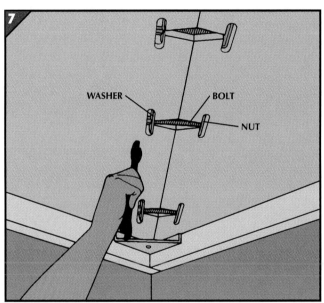

8. Caulking the backsplash.

To prevent water seepage between the countertop and the wall, fill the gap between the top of the backsplash and the wall with a bead of caulk. It is not necessary to seal the ends of the backsplash.

A Ceramic Tile Countertop

Durable glazed tile is virtually impossible to scratch, stain, or scorch, and the shiny, nonporous finish provides a sanitary work surface. Standard $4\frac{1}{4}$-inch-square tiles and latex-based grout both come in a wide variety of colors.

Buying Tile: First, calculate the square footage of your countertop, then add 10 percent to allow for wastage when cutting tiles and in case you ever need a replacement. Measure the countertop edge to determine how many trim tiles you'll need, and note your requirements for special tiles—mitered pieces for inside corners and caps for outside corners. The top row of the backsplash requires bullnose tiles, including a pair of double-bullnose units for the ends.

The Layout: The most appealing design will satisfy three goals: uniform grout joints, a symmetrical arrangement around the sink, and no tiles less than 1 inch wide—they are hard to cut and unsightly.

Make a dry run using plastic spacers or the molded-in tabs on some tiles to provide $\frac{1}{8}$-inch grout joints. If that approach fails, try the suggestions at the bottom of the opposite page. You can make all the necessary cuts yourself to fit tiles around the sink and against the wall. The trim tiles, however, must be cut by a tile supplier.

Preparing the Countertop: Remove the sink, as shown on page 102, and the old backsplash. If removing the backsplash is impracticable, you can tile over it *(page 111)*. Fill any nicks or cracks in the countertop with wood putty, then sand it with coarse (60-grit) sandpaper.

If the counter overhangs the base cabinets, either glue and nail strips of wood to the underside to make the edge as deep as the trim tile, or cut off the overhang with a circular saw; set the blade to the thickness of the countertop and adjust the saw guide to cut it flush with the edge of the cabinets.

TOOLS

Framing square
Notched spreader
Tile nippers
Tile cutter
Tile sander
Rubber-faced grout float
Caulk gun

MATERIALS

Epoxy adhesive and solvent
Latex-based grout
Silicone caulk
Silicone-based grout sealant

SAFETY TIPS

Rubber gloves protect your hands when you are mixing and applying tile adhesive, grout, and sealant. Wear safety goggles when cutting tile to shield your eyes from flying chips.

LAYING OUT A DRY RUN

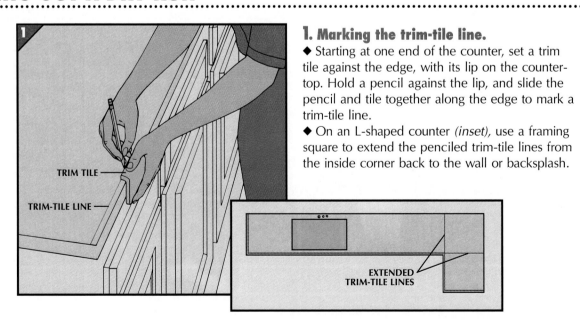

TRIM TILE

TRIM-TILE LINE

EXTENDED TRIM-TILE LINES

1. Marking the trim-tile line.

◆ Starting at one end of the counter, set a trim tile against the edge, with its lip on the countertop. Hold a pencil against the lip, and slide the pencil and tile together along the edge to mark a trim-tile line.

◆ On an L-shaped counter *(inset),* use a framing square to extend the penciled trim-tile lines from the inside corner back to the wall or backsplash.

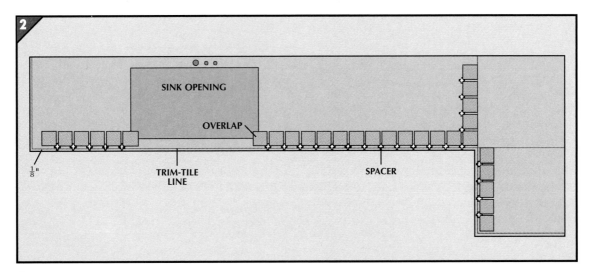

SINK OPENING

OVERLAP

$\frac{1}{8}$"

TRIM-TILE LINE

SPACER

2. Laying a dry run.

◆ Place two rows of tiles on the countertop, one of them $\frac{1}{8}$ inch—the width of a spacer tab—behind the trim-tile line, the other at right angles to the first and continuing to the wall. On a straight countertop, position the first tile $\frac{1}{8}$ inch inside the trim-tile line at the end of the countertop. For an L-shaped counter *(above)*, begin at the extended trim-tile line in the corner.

◆ Where a tile protrudes over the sink opening, measure the overlap and match it when positioning the first tile at the opposite side of the opening. Continue the dry run to within a tile width of the end of the countertop. Repeat the procedure for the other arm of an L-shaped unit.

◆ Place tiles along the front of the sink opening, working from the corners toward the center.

◆ Examine the dry run. If it requires tiles less than 1 inch wide to fit around the sink opening or to fill any gaps, widen the tile spacing *(below)*.

TRICKS OF THE TRADE

PENCIL MARK

JOINT GAUGE

Adjusting the Layout

One way to fix a dry run that calls for tiles less than 1 inch wide is to spread the tiles farther apart—the joints can be up to $\frac{1}{4}$ inch wide. If this approach fails, try marking the centerline of the sink opening on the countertop. Then center either a tile or a grout joint on the mark and work outward to the corners. Should neither of these tactics solve the problem, you may have to settle for an asymmetrical arrangement of tiles around the sink.

Spacers are of no help in achieving uniform grout joints if they are wider than $\frac{1}{8}$ inch. Instead, make a joint gauge from a 3-foot piece of $\frac{1}{4}$-inch wood lath. Without disturbing the dry run, lay the lath flush with a tile edge and mark its edge at the corners of several tiles *(left)*. Use this gauge to position tiles on the countertop, left to right and front to rear.

3. Working around the sink.

◆ Remove the tile next to the one overlapping each corner of the sink opening, and lay a framing square against the cabinet face as shown at right. Pencil a line on both sides of the opening from the front of the counter to the wall.

◆ Set a row of tiles along these lines, using spacers or the joint gauge to keep the joints uniform, then lay a row of tiles behind the opening flush against the wall.

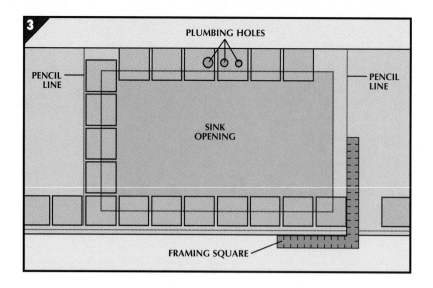

4. Marking the tiles for cutting.

◆ Wherever tiles extend over the sink opening, mark a cutting line on the underside by drawing the pencil along the edge of the opening *(far left)*. At the back of the opening, mark tiles to fit between the wall and plumbing holes in the countertop.

◆ For a row of partial tiles against the wall *(left)*, place a tile facedown on top of a full tile in the preceding row, edge against the wall. Mark both sides of the overlapping tile one joint width from the edge of the underlying tile, then join these marks across the face of the tile.

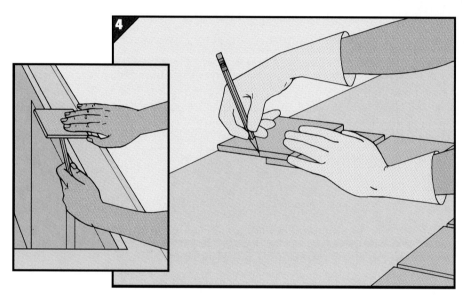

TWO TECHNIQUES FOR CUTTING TILE

A tabletop tile cutter.

◆ Set a marked tile on the padded base, lift the handle, and push it forward until the scoring wheel touches the tile's far edge.

◆ Then place the wheel on the cutting line, set the adjustable fence against the side of the tile, and tighten the thumbscrew. The fence helps hold the tile and simplifies cutting several tiles to the same width.

◆ Pulling up on the handle, slide it toward you to score the tile *(right)*.

◆ To break the tile, rest the heel on the tile and press firmly on the handle.

⚠ **CAUTION** *Cut tiles are sharp. Dull the edges with a tile sander, available from any tile supplier.*

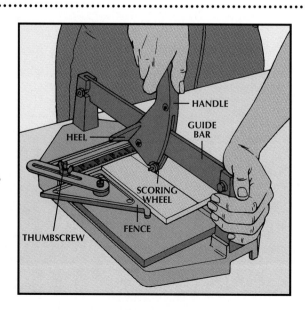

Irregular cuts with tile nippers.

◆ Position the jaws of the nippers to take a $\frac{1}{8}$-inch bite from the edge of the tile, then squeeze the handles to nip off a small piece of tile.

◆ Continue taking $\frac{1}{8}$-inch bites until you reach the cutting line.

SETTING TILES IN ADHESIVE

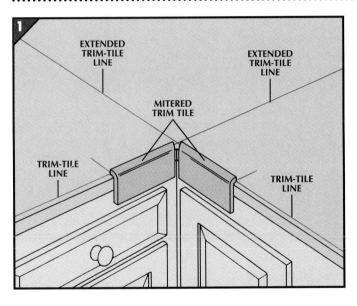

EXTENDED TRIM-TILE LINE

EXTENDED TRIM-TILE LINE

MITERED TRIM TILE

TRIM-TILE LINE

TRIM-TILE LINE

1. Setting the trim tiles.

◆ For an L-shaped counter (left), make two marks at the countertop edge, each a tile width from one of the extended trim-tile lines.

◆ Using a notched trowel, spread epoxy-based adhesive on both inside surfaces of a mitered-corner trim tile. Align the tile with the marks and the trim-tile line at the L's inside corner, and press the tile firmly in place without sliding it along the surface. Repeat for the other corner trim tile, then, using spacers or a joint gauge, proceed to both ends of the counter. Stick caps to outside corners, then continue to the walls with trim tiles.

◆ On a straight counter, start the row of trim with an outside corner cap—or with the tile at one end of a countertop that is set between walls or cabinets.

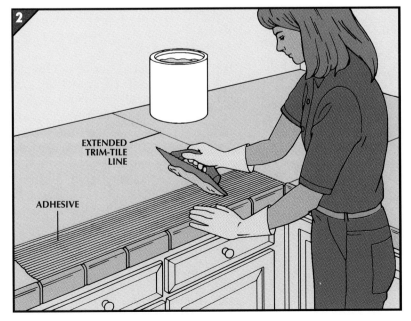

EXTENDED TRIM-TILE LINE

ADHESIVE

2. Spreading the adhesive.

◆ Starting at one end of a straight counter or the inside corner of an L-shaped counter, spread a band of adhesive one tile wide about 24 inches along the countertop.

◆ On a straight counter, start in one corner and align the edges of a square tile with a trim tile. Press it down firmly without sliding it across the adhesive. On an L-shaped counter, align a square tile with the mitered trim tile and the extended trim-tile line.

◆ Then set a row of tiles along the entire band of adhesive.

3. Laying surface tiles.
◆ Spread adhesive between the first row of tiles and the wall. Working from the edge of the countertop toward the wall, set a row of tiles along the edge of a straight counter or the extended trim-tile line of an L-shaped counter *(left)*.
◆ Continue to set tiles in diagonal rows until all the adhesive is covered.

4. Tamping the tiles.
◆ Level the tiles you have laid so far with a straight 2-by-4 about 18 inches long. Place the board facedown on the tiles and move it around, gently tapping it with a hammer to force protruding tiles into the adhesive. Wipe away excess adhesive with a solvent recommended by the manufacturer.
◆ Finish tiling the countertop, a section at a time.

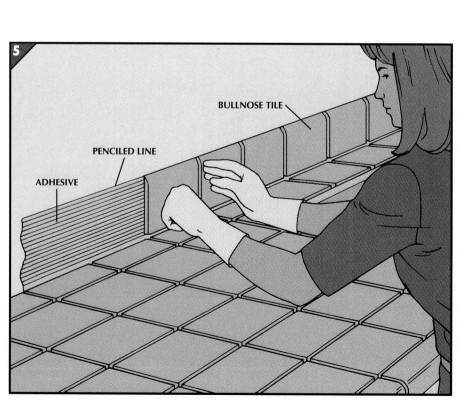

BULLNOSE TILE

PENCILED LINE

ADHESIVE

5. Making a backsplash.
◆ Mark the height of a bullnose tile on the wall at several points. Add the width of a grout joint to this mark, and draw a pencil line across the wall at this level.
◆ Spread a band of adhesive 24 inches along the wall between the countertop tiles and the pencil line. Set bullnose tiles into the adhesive, each with the curved edge at the line and the sides aligned with the corresponding tile on the countertop. Continue setting tiles along the length of the backsplash. At each end of the backsplash, set a double-bullnose tile—one with two rounded edges.
◆ Let the adhesive cure for 24 hours.

TILING AN EXISTING BACKSPLASH

Most laminate countertops have built-in back-splashes, typically $\frac{3}{4}$ inch thick and 4 inches high. If the backsplash cannot be detached easily, you can tile it to match the countertop.

The front face is covered with regular square tiles; measure and cut them two joint widths shorter than the backsplash height. In addition, cut two tiles to leave one joint width uncovered at the ends of the backsplash.

Cover the top of the backsplash with bullnose tiles, cut so that the rounded front edges are even with the faces of the vertical tiles. On the rectangular end of the backsplash, use a double-bullnose tile—rounded on two adjacent sides—with the rounded edges even with the top and front of the backsplash.

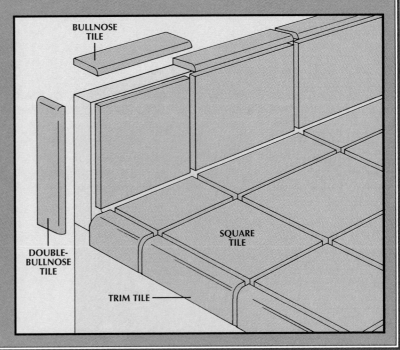

6. Grouting the counter and backsplash.

◆ Press twisted strips of newspaper into the joint between countertop and backsplash tiles to prevent grout from entering.

◆ Scoop grout onto the tiles, 1 cup at a time. Sweep the edge of a rubber-faced float diagonally across the surface several times to force the grout into the joints.

◆ Compact the grout in each joint with the edge of the float (above) so that the grout is slightly below the surface of the tiles.

◆ When all joints are filled, clean the float and sweep it across the tiles like a squeegee to remove excess grout. Wipe the surface with a damp sponge, and let it dry. Polish off any grout haze with a soft cloth. Caulk the joint between the countertop and the backsplash.

◆ Let the grout cure for three days, then spray the joints with a silicone-based sealer to prevent stains and leaks.

New Faces for Old Cabinets

One economical alternative to installing new kitchen cabinets is to reface the old ones. The job consists of replacing old doors and drawer fronts with new ones and veneering the cabinet frames to match.

Acquiring Materials: Supplies for the job are available through millworks, cabinetmakers, or firms that specialize in cabinet refacing. After choosing a style and finish for the new doors and drawer fronts, order veneer in a matching finish to cover the ends and faces of the cabinets.

Two kinds of veneer are required. Thin peel-and-stick veneer for the cabinet faces comes in sections that are 2 by 8 feet and are precoated with a pressure-sensitive adhesive. Veneer for cabinet ends is mounted on $\frac{1}{8}$-inch plywood and is available only in 4- by 8-foot sheets. Ask your supplier to cut the veneer for you slightly larger than the ends of your cabinets.

Things Not to Overlook: Besides the veneer, you'll want prefinished molding to trim the tops of eye-level

cabinets and the ends where they meet the kitchen ceiling and walls. To fill joints and nail holes, ask for a touch-up kit containing a wood crayon—a stick of filler that matches the finish on the veneer.

The face of many a cabinet extends $\frac{1}{4}$ inch beyond the ends, creating a void that must be filled before the ends can be veneered. For this purpose, purchase $\frac{1}{4}$-inch luan plywood, which is named for the tree whose wood gives the material a smooth surface ideally suited to adhering veneer.

TOOLS

Utility knife	Level
Hand roller	Circular saw with
Fine-toothed hand-	plywood blade
saw	Backsaw
Combination square	Miter box
Nail set	$\frac{1}{4}$-inch drill

MATERIALS

	Drawer pulls
	Drawer fronts
	Contact cement
	$\frac{1}{4}$-inch luan plywood
Doors	Medium sandpaper
Plywood-backed veneer	Clear lacquer spray
Peel-and-stick veneer	$1\frac{1}{4}$-inch finishing nails
Trim molding	Wood filler
Hinges	Wood crayon
Door handles	Felt or plastic bumpers

VENEERING CABINET ENDS

1. Preparing the cabinet frames.
◆ Remove drawers, doors, and hinges from the cabinet frames. Pry off any trim and save the pieces as guides for cutting new molding.
◆ Strip painted surfaces and fill nail and screw holes with wood filler. Sand the cabinets smooth, then wipe them clean with a damp cloth.
◆ If necessary, measure and cut pieces of $\frac{1}{4}$-inch luan plywood to fit between the stiles and the wall *(right)*. With a small paint roller, coat the plywood and cabinet ends with contact cement. Press the plywood to the cabinet and secure it with $\frac{1}{2}$-inch nails.
◆ Spray the cabinet exterior and plywood with three coats of clear lacquer.

2. Securing the veneer.

◆ Hold a piece of veneer against the end of the cabinet. Run a pencil along front and bottom edges of the cabinet to mark guidelines on the back of the veneer.

◆ With a circular saw, trim the piece about $\frac{1}{16}$ inch shorter and $\frac{1}{16}$ inch wider than marked.

◆ Coat the cabinet and the back of the veneer with contact cement. Press the plywood in place, with one edge against the wall and another even with the bottom of the cabinet.

◆ Sand the protruding edge of the veneer piece flush with the end stile *(right)*, then spray clear lacquer on the sanded edge. Recoat any sanded areas of the stile.

PEEL-AND-STICK VENEER AROUND OPENINGS

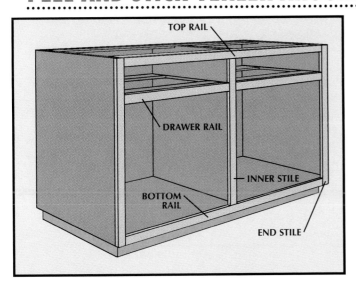

The best sequence.

The cabinet face is composed of vertical pieces, called stiles, and horizontal ones, called rails *(left)*. Using the technique shown below, veneer each piece individually, beginning with the end stiles. Cover top and bottom rails next, followed by inner stiles. Veneer drawer rails last.

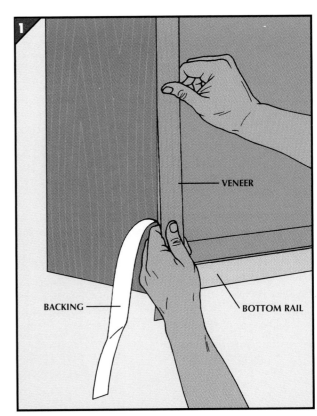

1. Veneering end stiles.

◆ With a straightedge and utility knife, cut two strips of veneer that are $\frac{1}{2}$ inch wider and 1 inch longer than the end stiles.

◆ Peel a few inches of backing from one strip and, with the grain running vertically, lightly press it against the stile, flush with the top. Working down the stile, continue peeling off the backing and pressing the veneer against the cabinet *(right)*. Cover the other end stile in the same way.

113

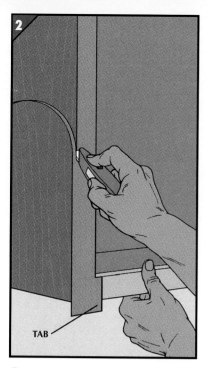

2. Trimming the veneer.

◆ Run a utility knife down the inner edge of each stile, then cut along the top of the bottom rail, leaving a small tab of veneer on the bottom rail.

◆ Next trim along the outer edge of the stile *(above)* and the bottom edge of the rail.

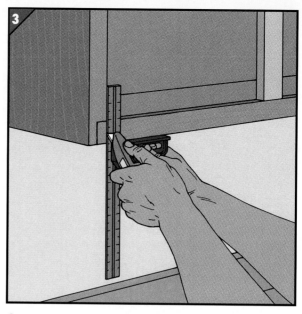

3. Covering the rails.

◆ Cut two strips of veneer $\frac{1}{2}$ inch wider than the top and bottom rails and long enough to overlap both end stiles.

◆ Press the veneer against the rails as described in Step 1, then trim the veneer along the top and bottom edges of both rails.

◆ Using a combination square as shown above, cut through the rail veneer and the tab of stile veneer at each end of the two rails. Remove the scraps thus formed, and press the rail veneer into place.

◆ Follow the same procedure to veneer first the inner stiles and then the drawer rails.

4. Finishing up.

◆ When all the peel-and-stick veneer is in place, run a hand roller along the stiles and rails to permanently bond the veneer to the cabinet face.

◆ Cut trim molding with a backsaw and a miter box to cover the joints that the cabinets form with the walls and the ceiling. Nail the molding to the cabinets with $1\frac{1}{4}$-inch finishing nails *(right)*.

◆ Sink the nail heads into the trim molding with a nail set.

◆ Conceal the nail holes—as well as joints between pieces of molding and veneer—with a wood crayon.

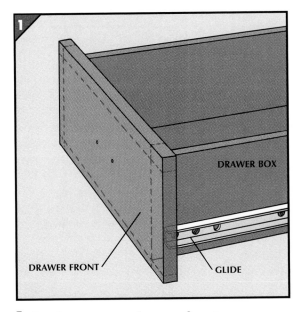

1. Putting on new drawer fronts.

◆ Remove the old drawer fronts if you can do so without damaging the drawer box. Otherwise, unscrew the drawer glides and trim each front flush with the drawer box *(dotted lines, above left)* using a fine-toothed saw. Reposition the drawer glides so that they are flush with the drawer front as shown above right, and drill two screw holes through the drawer front and the drawer box.

◆ Lay a new drawer front on the floor with the finish side down, and center the drawer box on it. Through the screw holes in the box, mark the front for pilot holes and drill them as shown on page 4. Then screw on the new front from inside the drawer.

2. Hanging new doors.

◆ Attach hinges to each door 2 to 3 inches from the top and bottom edges.

◆ With a helper holding the door in place, center it on the door opening and level it *(left)*. Then reach inside the cabinet and mark the frame for pilot holes where the hinges will attach to the cabinet frame. Drill pilot holes, and mount the door.

◆ Install the adjacent door by aligning it with the level on the one that is already in place.

◆ Mount the door and drawer handles and put felt or plastic bumpers on the inside of the doors and the drawers to protect the veneer.

Installing a Sheet-Vinyl Floor

If your kitchen floor is worn or damaged beyond repair, or if you just want a new look, you may want to consider using vinyl. Available in square tiles *(page 122)* or in large sheets, vinyl flooring comes in a wide variety of colors and patterns with a durable, no-wax finish. Vinyl is also easy to install; doing the project yourself will result in a significant cost savings.

One of the biggest advantages of vinyl is that it can usually be laid right over the existing floor. A variety of products are available to smooth and level the old surface in preparation for installation of a new floor. Talk to a salesperson when purchasing your new flooring, and read the manufacturer's instructions to determine what you need.

Measurements and Preparations: To calculate how much flooring you will have to buy, measure the dimensions of your kitchen floor at the widest and longest points in the room and add 6 inches at each wall for overlap. If you find you will need more than one sheet, note the width of the pattern repetition on the flooring you have chosen; it is usually printed on the back of the sheet. For example, if your pattern repeats every 3 feet, allow 3 feet of extra width when you buy the material.

Before beginning the installation, remove the shoe molding or vinyl wall base as shown on pages 20 and 22 and move appliances out of the kitchen so the new flooring can be laid underneath. Scoot these heavy items on a piece of hardboard to protect the floor.

The Finishing Touch: When the floor is in place, attach metal edging at the kitchen doorways to conceal the edge of the vinyl sheet.

TOOLS

Utility knife
Notched spreader
Rolling pin
Metal yardstick

MATERIALS

Vinyl-flooring adhesive
Seam sealer

CUTTING THE MATERIAL TO FIT

1. Rolling out the material.

◆ Let the material adjust to room temperature for an hour or so; then, if you are using more than one sheet, start in one corner and unroll the larger sheet from the longest wall of the room. Leave 6 inches of overlap at each wall.

◆ When you reach a large immovable object, such as a center island, you will need to leave 6 inches of overlap as you cut around it. Reach under the roll and unroll the sheet back toward the starting wall *(right)*. Push the unrolled section against the object and, about 6 inches above the floor, cut from the outside edge toward the center with a utility knife. When you are about 6 inches short of the vertical side of the object, cut back toward the starting wall; make this cut at least 6 inches shorter than the object's depth.

2. Fitting around a large object.

Lift the roll over the object and lower it to the floor on the other side. Holding the corner of the flap you have made in the sheet, cut at a right angle toward the outside edge of the sheet. This should give you a 6-inch overlap along all three sides of the object.

3. Reversing the roll.

◆ Unroll the sheet completely, then pull it back and reroll the sheet from the far edge as shown at left. The tightness of the inner part of the original roll compresses the pattern; unless the roll is reversed briefly, the pattern will be smaller in one part of the room than the other.

◆ Unroll the sheet again and press it into all corners, to the extent that its natural resiliency will allow.

4. Laying the second sheet.

◆ Before bringing the second sheet into the kitchen, measure the width of uncovered floor from the first sheet's edge to the opposite wall. Add 6 inches, plus the amount of overlap required to match the pattern.

◆ Unroll the second sheet completely in an area free of obstructions. Mark the above measurement on the sheet and cut. Reroll the sheet and bring it into the kitchen.

◆ Starting again from the longest wall, roll the second sheet out as far as the obstruction, then pull it over the first sheet until the patterns match (above). Cut and fit the second sheet around objects as you did the first, leaving 6-inch overlaps at the walls.

5. Trimming the edges.

Pull the second sheet off the first and out of the way. At each wall and object, cut the first sheet back to about 3 inches above the floor (left). Take care in making this cut—you are now close to the final trim.

BONDING THE VINYL TO THE FLOOR

1. Applying the adhesive.
Pull the first sheet halfway back upon itself. With a notched trowel, spread adhesive over the exposed floor as closely as possible to the walls and corners, but leaving bare a 6-inch strip along the line where the first sheet will meet the second.

2. Affixing the first sheet.
Lift the edge of the sheet high above the floor and slowly walk it back into place over the adhesive. Press it against the wall and into the corners as closely as its resiliency will allow.

3. Rolling out the bumps.
With a rolling pin, start from the center and roll the material toward each of its edges. Work slowly, and be sure to flatten any bulges or air bubbles in the vinyl's surface.

4. Making the final cuts.

◆ To crease the material, press a metal yardstick into the angle where walls or objects meet the floor. Then slice along the edge of the yardstick with a utility knife *(right)*. Make the cuts as straight and accurate as possible; shoe molding or wall base will cover errors up to about $\frac{1}{2}$ inch.

◆ Repeat Steps 1 through 4 for the other half of the sheet.

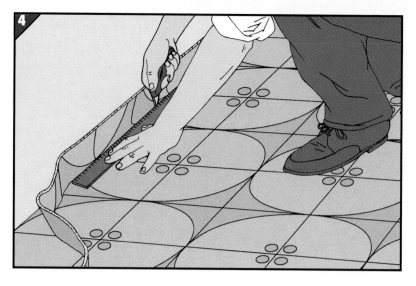

MATCHING THE PATTERN AT SEAMS

1. Cutting off the trim.

Place a metal yardstick along the overlap edge of the second vinyl sheet. With a utility knife, cut off the $\frac{1}{2}$- to 1-inch trim along this edge. On inlaid vinyl this trim is likely to be an extra-wide grout line; cut along the line so that its width matches the widths of the other grout lines in the pattern.

2. Matching the pattern.

Pull the second sheet over the first until the patterns of the two sheets match perfectly *(left)*. Note the pattern carefully to be sure the overlap continues the pattern in the same manner—a mismatched pattern will spoil the appearance of the finished job.

3. Cutting off the overlap.

◆ Place a metal yardstick along a grout line or other inconspicuous part of the pattern where the seam is less likely to show. Then, cut straight down through both sheets. Don't worry if it takes more than one pass with the knife to cut completely through the material; the important thing is that the cut be straight and clean. Remove the strips you have cut; the sheets should now abut tightly and have a perfect pattern match.

◆ Lay the second sheet as you did the first, trimming overlaps to 3 inches around objects and against walls.

◆ Spread adhesive to within 6 inches of the edge of the first sheet, and make a final trim along each wall and object.

4. Applying adhesive under the seam.

Follow the manufacturer's directions for sealing the seam between two sheets. Some vinyl flooring requires a special sealing adhesive below the sheets; with others you use regular adhesive underneath and seal the seam from the top.

◆ Pull back the butted edges on both sheets and spread adhesive over the bare floor along the entire length of the seam. Then press the sheets back in place, pushing the edges together until you get a tight fit.

◆ If seam sealer is called for by the manufacturer, proceed immediately to Step 5.

5. Sealing the seam.

Press the seam together with the thumb and fingers of one hand while applying seam sealer with the other. Wipe away any excess sealer immediately and keep off the seam for at least 24 hours.

The Versatility of Vinyl Tiles

Vinyl tiles offer virtually endless design possibilities for a kitchen floor. More often than not, tiles are laid in rows parallel to the walls of the room, but there are other options as well. You can, for example, create a diagonal checkerboard of contrasting colors, a pattern that can make a small kitchen look larger.

Learning from a Dry Run: Begin by snapping chalk lines *(page 123)* to divide the room into roughly equal quadrants, then lay tiles along the lines. For a simple parallel layout, begin the dry run at the inter-

section, and set tiles along each line to the walls. The dry run for a diagonal checkerboard, explained on these pages, is somewhat more complex. In either case, if the dry run would result in cutting very small pieces of tile in order to fill in along walls and elsewhere, start over with chalk lines in slightly different locations.

Laying the Tiles: When the dry run is satisfactory, prepare the old surface as described on page 116, then begin laying the tiles. Fill in a parallel pattern one quadrant at a

time, working from the center to the walls. A checkerboard pattern proceeds as shown beginning at the bottom of this page. Cut tiles to fit in spaces against walls and cabinets, taking care that the edges you cut form the outer edge of the floor, where they can be covered by baseboard.

When all the tiles are down, wipe up any excess adhesive, then press the tiles against the floor with a rolling pin or with a tile roller, which lets you do the work standing up. Keep traffic to a minimum for 48 hours to let the adhesive cure.

 **TOOLS**

 **MATERIALS**

Tape measure	Contour gauge	Vinyl tiles
Framing square	Notched trowel	Premixed adhesive
Chalk line	Scissors	Masking tape
Utility knife	Rolling pin	Paper

ESTABLISHING THE LAYOUT

1. Determining the starting point.
◆ Mark the center of the main kitchen doorway on the threshold. If there is no threshold to serve as a baseline, establish the center point on a line drawn between the corners of the doorframe.
◆ Position a framing square at the midpoint of the doorway *(right),* and draw a pencil line about 2 feet into the kitchen.

2. Marking the primary axis.

◆ With a helper, stretch a chalk line from the doorway to the opposite wall. Hold your end on the center point of the doorway, and have your helper move the other end to position the string directly over the pencil line on the floor.

◆ Holding the chalk line taut, with both ends pressed against the floor, lift the line directly upward a few inches and let go. It will snap to the floor, leaving a straight line of powdered chalk.

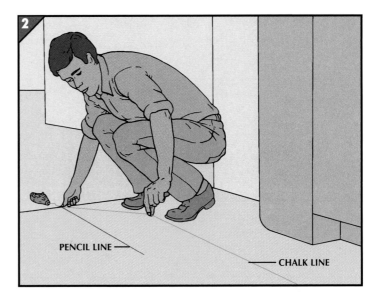

PENCIL LINE

CHALK LINE

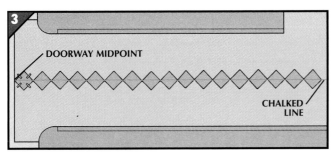

DOORWAY MIDPOINT

CHALKED LINE

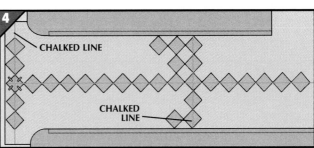

CHALKED LINE

CHALKED LINE

3. Starting the dry run.

◆ Place a tile diagonally along the chalked line with one corner at the point marking the center of the doorway. Tape it to the floor with masking tape.

◆ Set tiles of a single color along the chalked line until you come within 1 tile width of the wall (above).

4. Establishing secondary axes.

◆ At about the midpoint of the dry run—and wherever the room widens into an alcove or into a T or L shape—snap a chalk line the width of the room and perpendicular to the primary axis.

◆ Lay tiles of a single color along each of these secondary axes.

STICKING DOWN THE TILES

1. Laying the first tile.

◆ Note the working time of the adhesive, and make a conservative estimate of the area you can cover with tile in that time. Pick up all the tiles from the dry run, then pour equal amounts of adhesive on both sides of the chalk line near the doorway. Spread the adhesive evenly with a notched trowel to the chalk line but not across it.

◆ Holding a tile as shown at left, set one corner on the adhesive on the baseline at the midpoint of the doorway. Align the other corner with the chalk line and let it fall onto the adhesive. This tile must be absolutely straight, since it will determine the alignment of all the rest. Adjust the tile if necessary by nudging it gently.

2. Working across the floor.

◆ Begin by laying tiles of one color, corner to corner, along the baseline. Next lay a row of tiles of contrasting colors, creating the pointed array at left. Fill in the half-tile spaces at the baseline.

◆ Continue laying rows of tiles along the sides of the point to extend it to the far end of the room, alternating colors and aligning tile edges carefully.

◆ Where the room widens, use the zigzag edge of the tiled area as a baseline from which to extend the tiles to the left or right.

CUTTING TILES TO FILL GAPS

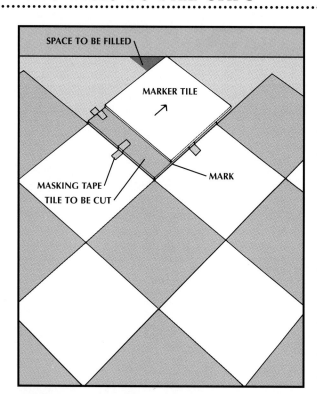

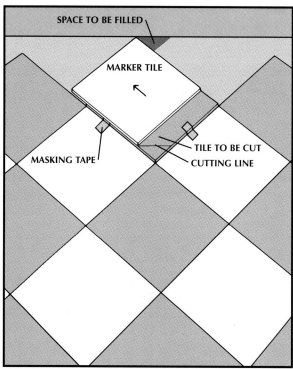

Making a triangular piece.

◆ Cut corners from tiles to fill small triangular spaces *(shaded area)* along walls. To do so, tape the tile to be cut—here a dark one—on a tile of the same color. Set a third tile on top to act as a marker.

◆ Slide the marker tile diagonally to the wall

(above, left). At the corner farthest from the wall, pencil a mark on the tile to be cut. Slide the marker tile diagonally in the other direction, and make another mark *(above, right)*.

◆ With a utility knife, cut along a straight line joining the marks, and set the triangular piece in place.

Filling a five-sided space.

◆ Tape the tile to be cut—in this case a light one—on top of a tile of the same color, then set a marker tile alongside it.

◆ Slide the marker tile diagonally to the wall, and mark where the corner farthest from the wall touches the tile to be cut. Set the marker tile on the other side of the tile to be cut and repeat.

◆ Use a utility knife to cut the tile along a straight line drawn between the two marks, and fit the five-sided piece in place.

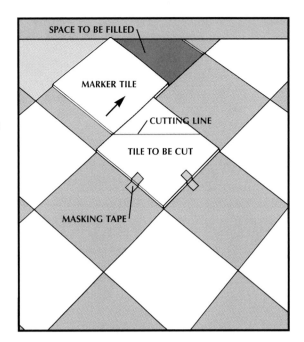

Cutting irregular shapes.

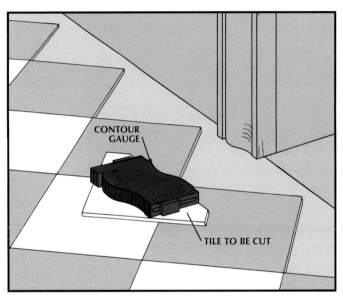

◆ To fit a tile against an irregularly shaped object, such as door molding, first cut a tile to fit the space to be filled as if the obstacle were not there.

CONTOUR GAUGE

◆ Then press a contour gauge against the irregular shape and part of the adjoining wall on either side, of it and lock the sliding fingers. Transfer the contour to the tile *(right)*.

◆ Warm the tile in a 200° oven for a few minutes, then cut it to shape with heavy-duty scissors.

Fitting tiles under a low overhang.

◆ To fit a tile against the base of an overhanging cabinet or appliance, tape a tile-size piece of paper to a nearby tile and place a marker tile atop the paper.

◆ Slide a corner of the marker tile under the overhang and against the base. Hold a pencil against the corner as shown at right, and slide the marker tile along the base, keeping the edges parallel to the tile seams.

◆ Transfer the pencil line on the paper to a tile of the right color, and cut the tile to shape. If there is not enough room below the overhang to trowel the adhesive onto the floor, spread a thin coat on the underside of the cut tile before fitting it in place.

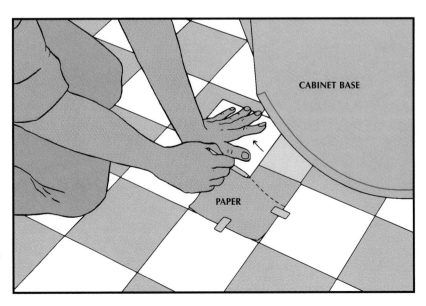

Time-Life Books is a division of Time Life Inc.

PRESIDENT and CEO: John M. Fahey Jr.

TIME-LIFE BOOKS

MANAGING EDITOR: Roberta Conlan

Director of Design: Michael Hentges
Director of Editorial Operations:
  Ellen Robling
Director of Photography and Research:
  John Conrad Weiser
Senior Editors: Russell B. Adams Jr.,
  Dale M. Brown, Janet Cave, Lee Hassig,
  Robert Somerville, Henry Woodhead
Special Projects Editor: Rita Thievon
  Mullin
Director of Technology: Eileen Bradley
Library: Louise D. Forstall

PRESIDENT: John D. Hall

Vice President, Director of Marketing:
  Nancy K. Jones
*Vice President, Director of New Product
  Development:* Neil Kagan
*Associate Director, New Product Devel-
  opment:* Elizabeth D. Ward
*Marketing Director, New Product Devel-
  opment:* Wendy A. Foster
Vice President, Book Production: Marjann
  Caldwell
Production Manager: Marlene Zack
Quality Assurance Manager: James King

HOME REPAIR AND IMPROVEMENT

SERIES EDITOR: Lee Hassig
Administrative Editor: Barbara Levitt

Editorial Staff for *Kitchens*
Art Directors: Kathleen D. Mallow
  (principal), Christopher M. Register
Picture Editor: Catherine Chase Tyson
Text Editor: Jim Lynch
Associate Editors/Research-Writing: Dan
  Kulpinski, Terrell Smith
Technical Art Assistant: Sue Pratt
Senior Copyeditor: Juli Duncan
Copyeditor: Judith Klein
Picture Coordinator: Paige Henke
Editorial Assistants: Amy Crutchfield,
  Renée Wolfe

Special Contributors: John Drummond
  (illustration); William Graves, Craig
  Hower, Eileen Wentland (digital illustration); Chris Hoelzl, Tom Neven, Peter
  Pocock, Glen B. Ruh, Eric Weissman
  (text); Mel Ingber (overread and index).

Correspondents: Elisabeth Kraemer-Singh
  (Bonn), Christine Hinze (London),
  Christina Lieberman (New York), Maria
  Vincenza Aloisi (Paris), Ann Natanson
  (Rome).

PICTURE CREDITS

Hardcover and Frontispieces: **Cover:** Pho-
tograph, Renée Comet; Props courtesy
Moen Incorporated; Art, Tyrone Taylor
and Patrick Wilson/Totally Incorporated.
7: Photograph, Renée Comet; Art, Ty-
rone Taylor and Patrick Wilson/Totally
Incorporated. **29:** Photograph, General
Electric; Art, Doug Chezem. **63:** Photo-
graph, Wood-Mode Incorporated; Art,
Tyrone Taylor and Patrick Wilson/Totally
Incorporated. **93:** Photograph, Renée
Comet; Prop courtesy The Home Depot;
Art, Tyrone Taylor and Patrick Wilson/
Totally Incorporated.
Soft-cover: Photograph, Renée Comet

Illustrators: James Anderson, Jane P. Ander-
son, Jack Arthur, Terry Atkinson, George
Bell, Frederic Bigio, Laszlo Bodrogi,
Roger Essley, Charles Forsythe, Gerry
Gallagher, William J. Hennessy, Elsie J.
Hennig, Walter Hilmers, Jr., Fred Holz,
John Jones, Al Kettler, Dick Lee, John
Martinez, John Massey, Joan McGurren,
Eduino J. Pereira, Tyrone Taylor/Totally
Incorporated.

Photographers: **End papers:** Fred Sons. **10:**
Renée Comet. **19:** Renée Comet. **31:**
Renée Comet. **47:** Steve J. Romanik, In-
ternational Approval Services. **55:** Renée
Comet. **83:** Porter-Cable Power Tools.
96: Renée Comet. **97:** Fred Sons. **125:**
Fred Sons.

ACKNOWLEDGMENTS

Christopher Baldwin, Middleburg, Va.;
John Chapski, Porter-Cable Corp., Jackson,
Tenn.; William Collins, Reston, Va.; Terry
Cooper, Cabinetpak Kitchens, Silver Spring,
Md.; J. Paul De Boek, Kitchen Face Lifts,
Sterling, Va.; Ed De La Vergne, Cabinet
Facers of Virginia, Reston, Va.; Feeny Man-
ufacturing Company, Muncie, Ind.; Carol
Gore, Middleburg Millwork, Middleburg,
Va.; Alice Herrold, Wood-Mode, Inc.,
Kreamer, Pa.; Scott Keener, Cabinet Facers
of Virginia, Reston, Va.; Larry Knapp,
Formica Corporation, Cincinnati; Eddie
Lichliter, Kitchen Face Lifts, Accokeek,
Md.; Sandra W. Lunte, KraftMaid Cabi-
netry, Inc., Cleveland; Mark Market, The

Home Depot, Alexandria, Va.; Deborah
Nelson, Rev-a-Shelf, Inc., Jeffersontown,
Ky.; Chuck Pfeiffer, Trible's, Inc., Spring-
field, Va.; Allen E. Pfenniger, Moen Incor-
porated, North Olmsted, Ohio; Mac Price,
Freelance Appliance Service, Inc., Fort
Washington, Md.; Progress Lighting,
Philadelphia; Quality Doors, Duncanville,
Tex.; Ridgid Tool, Elyria, Ohio; Robert St.
Clair Jr., St. Clair Appliance Distributors,
Inc., Alexandria, Va.; Ralph Sorrentino,
Kitchen Face Lifts, Blasdell, N.Y.; Wayne
Sorrentino, Kitchen Face Lifts, Sterling, Va.;
John Sullivan, Falls Church, Va.; Theresa
Szalkowski, International Approval Services,
Cleveland; Bill Taylor, Formica Corporation,
Cincinnati; Joe A. Teets, Fairfax County
Adult Education Program, Falls Church,
Va.; John Troxell Jr., Wood Mode Fine Cus-
tom Cabinetry, Kreamer, Pa.; Michael S.
Warlick, The Home Depot, Alexandria, Va.

Third printing. Printed in U.S.A.
Published simultaneously in Canada.
School and library distribution by Time-Life
Education, P.O. Box 85026, Richmond,
Virginia 23285-5026.

TIME-LIFE is a trademark of Time Warner
Inc. U.S.A.

**Library of Congress
Cataloging-in-Publication Data**
Kitchens / by the editors of Time-Life
Books.
p. cm. — (Home repair and improve-
ment)
Includes index.
ISBN 0-7835-3854-5 (hardcover ed.)
ISBN 0-7835-3855-3 (soft-cover ed.)
1. Kitchens—Remodeling—Amateurs'
   manuals.
I. Time-Life Books.
II. Series.
TH4816.3.K58K587 1994
643'.4—dc20   94-20347